The LinkedIn® For Sales and Marketing

By: Scott Aaron

Published by

Linked Leads Publications
Marlton, NJ

www.scottaaron.net

Contents

Acknowledgments

A project like this can never be done alone, and for that reason, there are some people I want to thank. First, I want to thank my parents, my sister Blair, my brother Jason, my incredible nieces Sia and Pepper Anthony, Andi, and my extended family and friends for always believing in me during the good and bad times and for always being present. I love you very much.

To all the wonderful clients who have invested in me so I can invest back into them, thank you for being amazing clients, inspirations, and friends. I am confident I have gotten even more from those trainings than anyone can imagine.

To my inner circle of close friends, thank you for always being willing to listen and help me through this journey called life. Your love and support have been instrumental, and I thank you and honor you.

To you who are reading this collection of wisdom, takeaways, and business growth strategies, thank you for your support. I hope this book blesses you as much as it has me.

To my writing coach, mentor, and content driver Brian K. Wright, thank you so much. This book, content, and project could not have been implemented if it wasn't for you. Thank you for your constant contact, wisdom, and advice as the book has come to fruition. Forever grateful for you and your guidance!

To my incredible son Taylor, thank you for always showing me the importance of being a kid at heart, having fun, taking risks, and loving life to the fullest. You bring joy and light to my life and all those lucky enough to know you. I love you, buddy, and I am so thankful and blessed to be your father and have you as my son!

And finally, to my fantastic wife, best friend, and "partner in crime," Nancy, for giving me the confidence, love and, seeing me through many challenges, obstacles, bumps, bruises, and giving me the desire to make a lasting impact on the world. Without having you in my life, I would not be who I am today. Thank you so much for everything, and I love you with all of me.

Foreword

Many dream of having a career not tied to a boss, time constraints, or lack of freedom. With so many choices, network marketing is a viable way to create income for many. Occasionally, you find a book that can help take your network marketing business to greater heights.

The *LinkedIn® Book for Sales and Marketing* is that book.

I met Scott Aaron several years ago online, and as I got to know him and his work, I realized what a vast and fantastic heart he must help people with. As I followed him on LinkedIn®, I noticed that he is very active on that platform—as he should be!

And so should you.

Scott takes us on a step-by-step journey to creating a thriving source of leads and sales for any online marketing business using LinkedIn®. If you don't use anything else, you can create a lucrative income using that alone.

He shows you how to create a profile that will entice people to connect with you, generate leads, create messages that grab attention, and most importantly, follow up with past leads.

If you have doubts about whether Scott is the go-to LinkedIn® mentor to work with, check out his testimonials on his LinkedIn® profile. There are more than 475 of them, some of which are included in this book.

While Facebook® is the platform where most people spend their time, you might be surprised that your best clients might not be there. Scott explains why that is the case.

If you want to not only start your business but also build it to greater heights than you thought possible, buckle up for the ride. What most people lack is a clear battle plan on a day-by-day basis.

You will find that here.

Not only is your battle plan here, but it is being taught and explained to you by a master of his craft. Learn everything you can from Scott Aaron, and even consider reaching out to him privately after you are done.

He also provides an abundance of case studies of people like you who made it happen, and if you use everything Scott teaches, you can change your life.

Read and apply what you see here; you won't regret it.

All the best,

Brian K Wright, Host of Success Profiles Radio and publisher of Success Profiles Magazine

Chapter One

Why LinkedIn® And How It All Began for Me

Congratulations on your wise decision to purchase this book. You are clearly interested in building a thriving and dynamic business using LinkedIn®. Many people dream of building a business and creating financial independence for themselves.

However, many don't go all-in—for many reasons.

Why would someone fail at business? For some, it's because they didn't pick an opportunity or create something that fully resonated with who they are but were chasing the promises of making gobs of money. Doing something ONLY for the money is usually a prescription for failure because negative energy gets attached to that, and people sense it.

For others, they fail because they didn't receive suitable training. Most "influencers," companies, business owners, and online coaches mean well and try to help as many people as possible. Still, those organizations and individuals are typically concerned about teaching the basics and just closing another sale.

I am always asked how I ended up using LinkedIn® in the first place. Well, that, my friends, is a critical story. I was always a traditional brick-and-mortar business owner in the health and wellness industry, owning multiple fitness clubs, splitting my time as a personal trainer, certified sports nutritionist, and corporate wellness speaker. I only had so many hours in the day to grow my business, and when your entire calendar is full of appointments, that will keep you working "in your business" and not working "on your business."

It could have ended up being a recipe for disaster as I was 33 years old, tired, burnout, unmotivated, and wondering what my next step would be. Someone asked me an interesting question. They asked, "if you got sick or injured and could not train people anymore, or your company went under, how would you earn income, and in what manner would you be able to do it? First, I had never been asked this question before. Second, it got the wheels turning in my brain for the first time in ages. Before that question, I had spent the last 15 years and 80+ hours a week running on the "treadmill of life."

My day would start at 4 am, so I would have time to get ready and get to the gym by 5 am. Once there, I would train clients every hour until nine o'clock at night. That was my life. That was my daily routine. That was the only way I knew how to earn money and grow my business. The more clients I trained, the more money I made. I was officially working harder and not working smarter. Going back to the original question my friend asked me, now that I was thinking about my "business mortality," I started thinking about other ways to create income, impact, and build a life I loved.

Shortly after this impactful conversation with my friend, I found myself in San Diego, California, at a personal development event. As I sat there listening to some incredible speakers who were sharing their knowledge, wisdom, and things that they had done on their path to achieving their success, there was a point in the conference where the host of the event welcomed some of the top entrepreneurs onto the stage to share some of their journeys. He asked each of them the same question, "How many conversations has it taken you to get your business to where it is today?" That was a very off-the-wall question because I would never have thought to ask about that aspect of a business. But it became abundantly clear when everyone grabbed that dry-erase marker and walked over to the whiteboard, with each of them writing conversation numbers that all exceeded 5000; I needed to re-think how I was approaching my online business.

Sitting there, I thought about what I was doing to move my business forward. I had a couple of revelations. The first revelation was understanding that I needed to start improving what I was doing in the online space. I only had so much bandwidth for meeting clients face-to-face but also networking with people belly-to-belly. I needed to create more flexibility in the way I was moving my business forward.

The second thing was understanding that social media would play a prominent role in helping my business get to where I wanted it to be. But a secondary question came up in my mind: "Which social media platform should I be using?" Should I use Facebook®? Should I use Instagram®? Those were the top platforms consistently and constantly being taught and spoken about. But as I sat there and thought about those two things, I remembered a social media platform I'd signed up for back in 2009 but did nothing with it, and that platform was LinkedIn®.

As I thought about the types of people that spend their time on Facebook® and Instagram® compared to the kinds of people that spend their time on LinkedIn®, I began to get the clarity that I needed to reopen that account and start looking at what LinkedIn® was all about.

I remember when I first logged back on in late 2013. It changed completely. It wasn't just a place where people went to look for a job or get recruited. It was a place where people could connect, network, and pass business back and forth. In diving deeper into the inner workings of LinkedIn®, I started by changing my profile, making connections quickly and abundantly, which led me to message people, and I even began to get responses back.

After a few days of this, I had phone call after phone call. Within a few weeks, my calendar began to fill up in a way that it had never filled up before. Now, as you can imagine, this was very exciting. A fire that had been dimmed for many years was lit and ignited inside me. Each day I would log onto LinkedIn® and go through the same process of utilizing LinkedIn®. Day after day and week after week, I would get the same results I was getting when I began: more connections, more conversations, more sales, and more business growth. This was my "lightbulb moment." I realized at that moment that I had created a flow and a system for anyone to maximize their use of LinkedIn®.

After acknowledging that this could be something big for the sales and marketing aspect of someone's business, I reached out to a friend of mine to share with him what had been working for me. When I got him on the phone, I mentioned how LinkedIn® was producing these drastic and impressive results for me and my business, and he should be doing what I was doing. I talked him through the specific nuances and ways I was leveraging LinkedIn® and what he should be doing. As we ended the conversation, he told me he would apply what he had learned from me and report back with his experience. Two weeks passed, and I got a text message from this friend. I remember this like it was yesterday. I grabbed my phone, opened a text from this friend, and the message read, "call me." That was it.

So, I called him and said, "what's going on?" He said, "Listen, whatever you shared with me the other day on how to leverage LinkedIn®, it 100% works". He said that after doing what I instructed him to do, he had booked over 14 discovery calls with ideal client prospects. He told me that in the 20-plus years of being in sales, he had never had that many calls in one week. He told me, "you should be teaching this. This is a gap and a hole in so many people's businesses that you can fill with this system you created".

There's an old saying that some of the most fantastic businesses, products, and services are created when the marketplace has a void or a gap causing people not to achieve a certain success. These businesses are formed when that individual creates something that solves many people's problems. That's precisely what I did with my LinkedIn® system.

I started to dive deeper into LinkedIn®, and as I did, more and more, it began to feel like a "parting of the Red Sea" moment. The quality of the conversations, connections and the overall user-friendliness of the platform made this a no-brainer for every business owner.

Not to mention, even more, head-turning statistics.

According to statista.com, following a dramatic increase of over 20 billion U.S. dollars from 2016 to 2017, total expenditure on training in the United States dropped from 93.6 billion in 2017 to **82.5 billion U.S. dollars in 2020.**

What does that statistic tell you? It tells me that fewer people are investing in themselves to learn proven strategies and techniques to grow their business, increase their leads, and close more sales.

That is a sad statistic—and it is entirely preventable!

If you want to build a thriving and impactful business, the starting place is knowing where to find quality people to talk to about your business.

Where do you find these people?

Many organizations and coaches teach that your warm market—your family and friends—is the best place to start (which has some validity). That might be a good idea if you haven't burned through all these people in previous businesses or opportunities.

But are your family and friends the best examples of your ideal client for what you have to offer? For many, the answer is no. This is because the true magic in building your online business happens outside our comfort zone (family and friends). The more you get uncomfortable, the more impact and progress you will see.

This begs the question once again: Where do you find these people interested in what I have to offer?

The answer may surprise you, but Forbes has said that if you are serious about building your business, using LinkedIn® is the best way to do it.

There are four significant reasons for this.

First, LinkedIn® is the best way to connect with ideal clients, and if you are looking to generate more qualified leads, you are fishing in the right pond. There are two ways that people get sales and clients in business. You can wait passively for people to come to you or actively look for other business-minded people who want to hear what you offer.

What I see many people doing right now is building their topsoil. Building on your topsoil means you have a lot of "low hanging fruit." However, to successfully market yourself on LinkedIn®, you must have a tree to your business.

To build your "business tree," you must make sure you grow the most important branch of your business. That branch of your tree is your ability to generate consistent leads. You must have a deep pool of leads because it's the foundation of your business. If you are only focusing on hoping people reach out to you, you will never build the strong roots of your business to support your tree. If you don't have strong roots, then this means that your tree will eventually collapse and die.

Therefore, generating quality leads will help you build the best business you can have that is strong, stable, and set up for success.

Suppose you are only using Facebook® and Instagram®. In that case, your chances of building an actual business are much smaller because those are designed to be SOCIAL and ENTERTAINMENT networks, whereas LinkedIn® is specifically designed for business networking, connecting, and collaborating.

The second reason why LinkedIn® is the most effective tool for lead generation, as Forbes.com explains, is that LinkedIn® is 277% more effective for unpaid and organic lead generation than Facebook®. It simply makes sense to use an effective lead generation tool because if you are looking to expand your business and have no leads, then you also have no business.

Posting and praying is not a strategy.

Reaching out to the same people repeatedly to convince them to work with you is also not a strategy.

You don't want to waste time and energy convincing someone to invest in your offering. You want to connect with people who already have a healthy money mindset. The average income for people on LinkedIn® is $100,000 per year, and you can have 30,000 connections there compared to only 5,000 contacts allowed on Facebook®. In addition, the average income someone makes on Instagram® and Facebook® is $30,000 or less.

The third reason using LinkedIn® is the best way to build your business is because it is ideal for thought leadership. For example, Lewis Howes got his start on LinkedIn® because he wanted to relate to other thought leaders. When you post content regularly, and people like and share it, you become an authority in your niche.

In addition, LinkedIn® is the only social media platform in the world where every Fortune 500 company has a presence. That is HUGE! This means there are compelling and influential people at your fingertips.

The final reason why LinkedIn® is the best way to build your business because it is the most effective content distribution platform for business-to-business. Forbes.com has said that LinkedIn® is 94% more effective for content distribution, which means people will see your content when you post it. Content is not only the messages you send to people who could be interested in your offering but also the posts that you make.

Many may argue that LinkedIn® is not the right place to build your business. The truth, however, is that when you decide to become a business owner and your ideal client is a professional, you will have a great chance of succeeding online using LinkedIn® over any other social media platform.

I can confidently say that if you want to make it in business and be someone who makes multiple six-figures on up, doing what you love, you must be on LinkedIn®.

You may wonder how to leverage this powerful platform to your advantage.

That's what this book is about.

You also may be wondering how to attract the right people, what to say to them in messages or on the phone, why groups are essential, and a whole host of other questions you may have.

Be prepared to learn a lot. Most people don't use LinkedIn® nearly enough simply because it is a mystery. I promise the top business owners are all using LinkedIn®, and I am here to show you how to do this correctly.

Let's begin!

Chapter Two

Creating Your Perfect Profile

What is the first thing people notice once they look you up on LinkedIn® or any social media platform?

The correct answer is your profile. People will decide to keep reading or not based on their initial impression of it. You only have two or three seconds to make a remarkable impression on your readers, or they will move on to someone else. If you don't grab attention immediately, the consequences could be a lost business opportunity, a missed referral or joint venture partnership, or a chance to speak to someone's group. Therefore, the initial first impression is critical.

The success I experienced with my LinkedIn® profile was trial and error. I didn't have a guide like this to inform the choices I should (or shouldn't) be making with my LinkedIn® profile. I don't want you to make the same mistakes I made initially.

The first thing you need is a welcoming, attractive background photo. You want your background photo to set yourself apart from other people, so this would not be simply a photo of you. The goal for this photo is for someone to be inspired as soon as they visit your page. In my current profile, I have a cover that shows me in action speaking at an event, in addition to my profile picture. If you don't yet have photos like that for your background, you can simply go to www.canva.com, type in "LinkedIn® Cover," and create your own that is branded to you and what you do. If you think of doing a Facebook® cover photo, for example, it serves the same purpose—it gives people insight as to who you are and what you do in a visually appealing way.

Next, you need a profile picture. This photo needs to be a clear professional picture of you. For example, I spent most of my career as a sports nutritionist and personal trainer. I was also an amateur bodybuilder. But that is not who I am anymore. I am now a coach, consultant, podcaster, and speaker. Therefore, when people see what I look like, I want them to know I am serious. This is who I am, what I represent, and what I stand for. It makes sense that you have a profile picture that describes you, fits you, and is you.

Below your profile picture, your name will appear. Then after that, you need a brief description. This is where viewers will get an immediate sense of who you are.

For example, if you're a financial advisor, marketing professional, real estate professional, business coach, or business consultant, you always want a powerful adjective to define your business.

You can use titles such as President, CEO, Founder, Creator of, Head Lady Boss, Head Honcho of, etc. I chose "Creator" because it felt good to me and should always accurately reflect who you are.

Many people put their LLCs in their profiles. I have an LLC, but it's nowhere found on my page because I want people to be connected to me, and that's it. Honestly, no one cares about your LLC, so there is no reason to include it.

Using keywords in your headline is vital for you to appear in more searches. When you appear in more searches, you have a more significant opportunity to connect with the right people who could benefit most from what you offer. You never put a "mission statement" as your headline. Many people have, "I help you create 7 + figures with ease and only have to work one day a week". That is not genuine. That is not authentic. And it is undoubtedly keyworded. Try something like (Coach | Business Consultant | Podcaster | Business Mentor).

One of the most frequent questions is about listing past positions in profiles. For example, "Should I list my previous job as a bartender even though I was there for a very short time? I would recommend it because later, I will show you how you can utilize those past experiences to your benefit by connecting the right people into your network.

Now, you also want to have the proper description for each of these listed positions. For example, mine could say, "I'm a Business Coach. I facilitate Online Marketers, Entrepreneurs, Financial Advisors, Real Estate Agents, Insurance Agents, Accountants, and Online Coaches on how to not only use the power of LinkedIn® to grow your business but how to implement social media to make yourself stand out without paying for leads or having to do funnels."

Next, you need to make sure that you have completed your summary. What I see many people do is that they either have a simple one-liner that does not go into depth about who the person is and what they do, or I see people with outdated information that has no reference to what they are currently doing.

The summary should be about WHY you do what you do, not what you do. To demonstrate, here's what I wrote: "As an experienced professional with two decades of work in leadership, sales training, lead generation, and the personal coaching industries, but most importantly being a husband and father to a beautiful little boy, I have learned the importance of creating the life that you deserve, but more importantly the mindset and loving each day with the utmost happiness.

I am passionate about spreading my mission of teaching others how to create human connections, build their brands and grow their wealth through the means of LinkedIn®.

I specialize in showing Entrepreneurs, Business Coaches,

Financial Services Professionals, and Online Marketing Professionals who are ready to fundamentally change the skills needed to shift the entire scope of their life by making new decisions that create the outcomes they deserve in life and for your business.

As an award-winning online marketer, 3x best-selling author, top podcaster, and speaker, I am the go-to specialist in converting traffic, establishing connections, creating income, and building personal brands on LinkedIn®.

Fully immersing myself in learning LinkedIn® and social media strategies, I quickly gained traction as a leader in generating significant results for other Entrepreneurs, Online Business Owners, Financial Advisors, Financial Planners, Network Marketing Professionals, and Business Coaches.

Being extremely motivated about helping others achieve success while building their network organically and without complicated and costly marketing tactics sets my coaching apart from others.

The program I created has helped thousands experience explosive business and monetary growth.

I am people-focused and result-driven, and my strategic approach to teaching others how to be creative in achieving wealth online and organic traffic changes the game when competing in a saturated digital world.

website for more info: www.scottaaron.net or email to contact me: scott@scottaaron.net."

So, you can take that and wrap it around yourself. For example, "In being a loving wife, mother, and educator, I have learned the importance of shaping people's mindsets. I now wake up with a growing passion for showing people how to live their life out loud and enjoy every moment simultaneously."

Now, it's essential to have every section filled out: Education, Volunteer Experiences, your Endorsements, Skills,

Recommendations, and Accomplishments. List as many things as you can that relate to your journey. Books you have written, articles you have been featured in, and awards you have won over the years will make your profile stand out.

Make sure you have an excellent, clean profile because it represents who you are. If you need an example, go to my LinkedIn® profile, and see what I have done. As I mentioned, you need to make this not about what you do—it's about why you do it.

Once you have a unique profile, you can start searching for groups to join on LinkedIn® so you can begin bringing people into your network.

We will discuss that in the next chapter.

SUCCESS STORY:

Jackie Serviss – Talent Strategist and Executive Coach

Jackie Serviss is a seasoned Human Resources Executive and Certified Executive Coach (CEC) with over a decade of assisting leaders in aligning people strategies and talent acquisition best practices to scale their organization. As a business owner and people strategist, Jackie leverages her leadership & integrated approach to drive strategy around talent planning & forecasting, organizational design, leadership development coaching, change management & staffing services.

With a passion for driving sustainable business growth through the power of people, Jackie is focused on strategic partnerships with leaders to drive results, build teams and create sustainable impact.

Facing disruptors in today's business landscape with a consistent lens on talent is at the forefront of all organizations. Jackie has developed a method to attract, develop and retain high-performance talent and is here to help you assess your needs and construct the right people strategy for you.

Jackie's experience working with companies like PepsiCo, Toll, and BlackRock, along with startup founders like Plexxis Software, Spitzen Limited, and Legacy Coaching, has given her the ability to create and produce attainable organizational talent plans that can scale up or scale back with ease. If you are trying to figure out what to do to grow the fantastic talent on your team, or attract the best talent into your company, connect with Jackie today to assess how best to get started.

"Hey there, my name is Jackie Serviss, and I am a business strategist, transformational coach, and speaker. My former life was as a corporate executive, and I've recently transitioned into being an online coach and building an online business, which is how I came across Scott Aaron.

You know, Scott has not only been my LinkedIn® coach, but he has also been my strategic coach and helped me see all facets of my business in a new light. It has been an absolute honor working with Scott, and I'll tell you, in the multiple weeks that we've worked together, his systems and how he explains things to you are simple and to the point and land you new clients.

In the first couple of weeks, I had a couple of new clients coming to my door, and that is all from the system that Scott teaches. So, Scott, a good friend and a dear coach, thank you so much for everything and for teaching me LinkedIn®".

Learn more about Jackie at http://jackieserviss.com/

Key Takeaways:

- Your profile is the first thing a new contact will see. It only takes seconds for someone to decide whether to connect further, so make it memorable and impactful.
- Use clear and professional photos of yourself. People want to put a face to what they are reading.
- Use power adjectives to describe who you are.
- Your summary is critical because it gives you a chance to tell people WHY you do something, not simply what you do.
- Fill out every section. Remember, your profile is designed to tell people how they can benefit from being connected with you—it's not a generic, boring resume.

Bonus: As a gift from me to you, please go to www.scottaaron.net and claim your free infographic about the best way to set up your profile on LinkedIn® so you can get started quickly and easily.

Chapter Three

Using The Search Engine And Groups To Build Your Network

Let's talk about laying down the foundation for joining the right kind of groups, as well as how we can connect your past and present to searching for the suitable types of people who would be most likely to accept your connections so you can start building your network. Groups get a bad rap on LinkedIn®. So many say, "they don't work," "they are a waste of time," and "people just sell and pitch all day long." To a certain extent, that is true. But I will respectfully disagree that they don't hold any value. They do, and I am going to explain why.

Later, we'll discuss how you can connect with people, two different methods you can use to communicate with people, and how to keep track of all that. This is important because you want to ensure that those people you're searching for and now connecting with are working for you and are suitable for your business.

With that in mind, let's talk about groups. On your main profile page, in the upper right-hand corner, you will notice a square grid with the word "Work" underneath it. You will also see a down arrow next to it. This is where all your groups are stored. Now, if you're not in any groups, I will show you how to join them. For example, my background includes wellness, coaching, podcasting, marketing, and mindset. Therefore, most of my groups have to do with those areas of business—things that relate to me. You don't necessarily want to join groups based on how many people are in them because those people may not be your ideal audience.

The reason you join groups is to find YOUR audience. Find the right groups with the right people in them so you can build your business.

You could search for groups in the same way that you would search for people. If I was searching for podcasters but wanted to search for podcasting groups, I can use the search bar and type "podcaster," and then it will allow me to filter what I want. In this case, I want "Groups." If I find a group called the Podcasters Network, I can select it and ask to join. Some groups you will instantly get access to, and others have a moderator that, in time, will accept your request to join.

Let's say you're a business coach and want to connect with more people in coaching; you can type in "Business Coach Groups." It will automatically go to groups, and you will find some coaching groups to join. You can also type in "real estate groups" and see a group called "Real Estate Agents Group." If you're an accountant, search "accountant groups." You would find, for example, Accountant-Lawyer Alliance, ALA. Let's say you want to connect with bartenders instead. You can search "bartender," "bartending jobs," or "bartending mixologist," and you would find thousands of people. The great thing about groups is that these are people whom you are not directly connected within your network that you can still connect with, which is a fantastic thing.

It's crucial to search for the "right" people. I always tell people that on LinkedIn®, you want to connect with the mirror image of yourself (your ideal client avatar). You don't want to search and connect with just anyone. You want to be able to search and connect with people who would be most relatable to you, get the most value from what you have to offer, and could network with to gain even more business opportunities. When I'm on LinkedIn®

conducting searches for myself, I make sure I'm searching and connecting with podcasters, business coaches, business consultants, and course creators—and I'll show you how I do this.

If I want to be broad, I'll type in "podcaster" and click on "People." Then you always want to make sure that you click "Second Connections," and people always ask, "Why?". First connections are already your connections, so you don't need to filter them out because you are already connected to them. Second connections are your connections' connections; third connections are your second connections once removed, which means that third connections are your first connections' connections' connections. To get to the third, you need to either pay for premium or know the person's email—and I don't pay for Premium. It's not that I don't believe in it, but I think you can stay within the tight niche of the general network you have right here and work off that without paying for Premium. Whether you want to pay for Premium or not is up to you, but I have not found a need for it.

I always filter by second connections. So, when I searched, I just mentioned that it brought back 49,000 people. That's a good number, but the value in this is finding specific connections. I can pursue this search further and type in "podcaster, course creator." Again, it's someone who's just like me. That search result moves from 49,000 down to 3,600. This simply proves that the more specific you get with your searches, the more specific you will get with the type of person you bring into your network.

I can go even one step further. I can add "business coach" to that search, so now my search is for "podcaster, course creator, business coach." The result is now 16 people who are just like me. Now, if I adjust the search, I can get rid of "podcaster" and just do "course creator, business coach," which brings 152 people. I can do "podcaster, business coach" and get 37 results, or just "business coach" by itself and get 16,000. You must play around with the types of people you want. Now that was a search I did for myself; your search terms might differ.

As another example, let's say you are currently a business consultant, but you were an HR coordinator before consulting. If your target client is burnt-out professionals like you, your search could be "business professional, Human Resources" and yield 570 results. If you searched for "HR, Coordinator," you would get 355 results. Now, if you want to get specific and incorporate coaching and mentoring into your search, you can do "HR, Coach" and get 11,000. You can also search for "Human Resources, business mentor" because you're looking for someone like who you were as an HR professional. Still, you're also looking for someone potentially interested in coaching or mentoring. The key is being very, very specific about whom you search for.

In chapter four, I'm going to get more in-depth on the searching and connecting technique, how often you should search, how many searches you're allowed, other ways to connect, and how to keep track of those new connections as they come in. Then in chapter five, I'm going to wrap up with exactly how and what kind of message you can send, two different types of messages, some of the objections you're going to get, and how to set up phone calls to connect with the people you find.

Success Story:

Jeremiah Campbell, Owner of Brickworks LLC:

Jeremiah Campbell has been actively involved in residential and commercial masonry contracting since 2004. He started as a laborer and worked his way up into an owner/operator of Brickworks. From 2004-2007 every job was sold and installed by Jeremiah, and by 2008, he took more of A management role, influencing others and showing them his leadership, knowledge, and community.

He works hard to ensure. Brickworks standards are far above the norm to deliver excellent service. Jeremiah holds the following certifications: CSIA, CCP, CCR, HeatShield, historically accurate mortar, lime mortar, and residential builder's license. He has worked for hospitals, schools, corporations, historic landmarks, governments, police stations, city halls, etc.

On top of his business, he and his wife Mallory have an incredible podcast called "Destined to Be."

They believe everyone deserves to live a life unstuck. Mallory and Jeremiah have always dreamt of working together. They decided it was time to take a leap of faith, and with the help of some divine timing, their businesses and podcast took shape.

They've been married since 2011, and are raising two boys, while still making time for each other. Focusing on improving their mental wellness can lead other couples and individuals to do the same in their lives. They strive to teach and offer everyday practices to help you to become un-stuck, design the life you want, and help you become the person you are destined to be. They are building a community of like-minded and like-hearted people and want to invite you to be a part of the family!

"Hey, Scott, I just wanted to send you this message in appreciation. I got a letter yesterday about a deal we've been working on that would have been impossible if not for your LinkedIn® strategy. I hired you about three or four months ago for LinkedIn® coaching. I never had any LinkedIn® presence. I made a LinkedIn® account. You helped me optimize it; you taught me how to reach out. So, this contract was the biggest in my company's history.

We've been in business for this will be our 15th season. So, it's the biggest contract. It's entering us into an entirely new world of our business. I am a mason contractor, and I reached out to you for help, and you taught me how to target my general contractors, architects, project managers, and property managers. With that help, we closed the biggest deal. A $300,000 contract!!

I'm so grateful to you. Anybody that is in the process of or thinking about hiring him as a LinkedIn® coach? It's so worth that. Love you, Scott. Thanks."

Learn more about Jeremiah at:
https://www.chimneyrepairdetroitmi.com/
or
www.destinedtobepodcast.com

Key Takeaways:

- Join groups to find YOUR audience, not just to accumulate connections who don't share common interests
- Be specific in your searches to find highly targeted connections. It's better to connect with a smaller, highly focused group than a large group with fewer things in common with you.
- Filter by second connections. These are individuals who are connected to people you are already connected to. It's a great way to build your network.

Chapter Four

Exploding The Reach Of Your Network

So far, we have discussed setting up your profile correctly to make it as attractive as possible for potential connections. We also discussed laying down the foundation and the groundwork for searching for the right groups to join and finding the suitable types of people to bring into your network.

Now let's talk about strategies you can incorporate to make the most of your searches.

There is a method to my madness regarding how I grew my connections from 500 to 27,600 in 4 years, how I get as many conversations per week as I require, and how I close anywhere between two to four sales per week, just on LinkedIn®.

I will show you precisely what you need to do daily to make this happen. I'll go through it slowly because there is a process, and I will explain some tools you need to make this work effectively for you.

First things first. Start from your home screen.

The methodology begins with sending no more than 100 connection requests per week. LinkedIn® will block and potentially remove you from the platform if you violate this too often. So that could be 20 connections five days per week or 14 connections seven days a week. The choice is yours. This is imperative because people won't know who you are if you don't reach out. You can't expect people to reach out to you first. Now when I say reach out to 14 to 20 connections daily, that doesn't mean that all of them will accept your request. That's 14 to 20 people you're looking to connect with who are the right fit for you and will enable you to grow an extensive network. With that being said, I'm going to take you through my daily habit of what I do to connect with my network.

I'm a big believer in being genuine and authentic and not having to pay for leads if it's not necessary. I also believe everyone is on LinkedIn® to network for the proper purpose, especially for a business that requires human connection to move it forward. We are here to create authentic conversations with real people to grow an entire network for your business.

The first thing to do when you wake up in the morning is to have a marker of where your most recent connections are. You'll need to click on "My Network." This is going to bring up a couple of different things. It's going to bring in some people who are looking to connect with you. It's also going to bring up the "People You May Know" section, which I'm going to get into. But the most important thing is your connections, and what you're going to do is you're going to click on "connections." What this is going to do is going to bring up all your connections in sequential order, and it is going to show you "Most Recently Added."

The idea is to keep track of your new connections and discover who they are because your new connections are your new leads. Now, for example, we're going to pretend that you went to "My Network" and clicked on "See All." Let's say that Jon Dough was your most recent connection. So, what you're going to do is get out a piece of paper, and you're going to write on the top "Most Recent Connection" and add rows for Monday, Tuesday, Wednesday, etc., and then you're going to put Jon's name for whatever day you found him.

So, this is going to be your marker. You need to have a line in the sand to know precisely where you need to work up from. Your most recent connections are at the very top. Your older connections that you've connected with are below them. Now you have your marker.

Here's my connecting style. I do specific searches on Monday and Friday because with the free version of LinkedIn®; you are only allowed 12 to 15 searches per month. If you've been on LinkedIn® and tried doing searches before, you will get messages that say that you're getting close to your commercial limit for your searches. Trust me; I went through that. I was searching way too much.

So, Monday and Friday, you're going to do specific searches. Your other connections will come from the "My Network" area on Tuesday, Wednesday, Thursday, Saturday, and Sunday. These are the people you may know, and they represent your first connections-first connections, which is your network. With the free version of LinkedIn®, you can tap into them immediately.

Let's run through an example. If it's Tuesday, I'm going to look for people that I can connect with that fit my description of the mirror image of me, whether it's a podcaster, someone that's my ideal client avatar, or even a power partner (someone who could introduce me to someone else) — and I'm very, very specific.

To review, on Tuesday, I go through my connections first thing in the morning, then define my marker, and I'm done for the day because I sent out my connections. On Wednesday morning, I go to my home page and recheck my most recent connections. Now, we're going to click on "My Network," then we're going to click on "my connections" on the left-hand side, and we're going to look through the list and find Jon. But now Jon is not on top anymore, because we notice, for example, that we have five new people. They now represent your brand-new leads and are your brand-new connections.

You then directly message them, and the next chapter will

discuss what you will say in more detail. Remember that once you identify your new leads, the only name you must write down is this first name at the top of the list because that's your new marker. Let's say the person's name is Nancy. The next time you receive new connections, Nancy is now your new marker, and every new connection above her name is a new lead.

Since it's Wednesday, this is one of your "my network" days, so you will use that section to send out your next batch of connections. You wake up Thursday, and you go back to "My Network," you go back to "See All," and you see who has appeared above Nancy, who was the person from the day before. So, this is a way to start accumulating leads. So, the first thing you always do is to get your marker and send messages, then the next thing you do is to get those subsequent connection requests out, and you're just going to windshield wipe back and forth between those activities.

This is the basis for what you're going to do. It's 14 to 20 connections every day. On Monday and Friday, you do specific searches. On Tuesday, Wednesday, Thursday, Saturday, and Sunday, you use the "My Network" section.

Every day, you're sending out those 14 to 20 connections. That's the activity that will build your pipeline consistently.

In chapter five, we'll go over messaging those brand-new people, what to expect with responses, what kind of scripts you can use that are genuine and authentic, and what you can say to them to get started.

Success Story:

Janis Thorton – Top Rated Golf Personal Trainer

Passions of mine include weight loss/general fitness and golf fitness. I used to work in cardiac rehab and the pharmaceutical industry for over 25 years combined. I am passionate about helping others get off medications and stay out of cardiac rehab. I've seen so much illness… it's time for wellness.

Another passion of mine is golfing, as I play 2-4/week. I always want to be able to help fellow golfers with their golf game. I'm greedy…I want people to play golf with me in my 60's, 70's, and 80's! JT Fitness and Golf will help you reach your fitness goals, whether losing weight or improving your golf game. You are exactly where you need to be!

Take your time back! Workout from home with fast and effectively online, individually designed, convenient workouts. Now you can find YOUR best self. Whether you want to improve your golf game or lose weight, these workouts are for you! Learn easy-to-use strategies for ultimate health and fitness.

For over three decades as a wellness professional and, more recently, being an online personal trainer, I have had two passions when it comes to life. One is helping those who are on a personal journey and those that love the game of golf. Both passions require empowering you from the inside out, so you reach your ultimate goals. But honestly, what inspires me most is being a loving wife and mother. I know the importance of showing up each day for those around you that mean the most to you. My mission is to impact people physically and financially and show those around me how amazing life can be when you truly see it that way. Whether you want to lose weight, improve your golf game, get stronger, look younger, have more energy, find time for exercise, or whatever your goals are, I'd love to guide you, so you feel your best.... because you deserve it. Not all personal trainers are created equal. I understand the mind/body battle that can sabotage your efforts. My professional training, combined with a compassionate approach, gives you a training companion in a no-nonsense way to build an environment for results!

"If you find yourself struggling with LinkedIn®, not sure what to say, whom to connect to, what to do with all these groups, I highly recommend working with Scott, I'm an online personal trainer, and I also do online marketing.

I'm like, I know I need to be on LinkedIn®. I know I want to grow my business. And where I was getting stuck was, what the heck, I could connect with people. But then, what do I do with all these connections? And once I started working with Scott, things began to change. So, for example, I had about 2300 connections when I started with him nine months ago. And now, I have over 3400 connections on LinkedIn®, which I got in less than nine months.

Also, I used to have literally 46 people viewing a post or viewing, my profile was very, very low. Now I'm up to 300, and I'm almost to 400. I'm someone who will do as much as Scott recommends. I work on LinkedIn® probably three to four days a week, instead of the five to six plus days he recommends. Now also, I will say this, I am that person that works better one on one. I know Scott has different programs for you to join, so I decided to go all in with working directly with him because I knew that if I had just to watch videos and do things on my own, I wouldn't do it. And that's where Scott comes in to help you.

So, if you are sitting on the fence, wondering what you should do, I highly recommend that you just take the leap, hire Scott, and have him handhold you on the weekly calls with him. That way, he can take you and your LinkedIn® to the next level so you can truly hit your goals.

I know we all want to grow our business with businesspeople who also want to do the business. Guess what? I have closed four clients through LinkedIn®. And I never knew them. I never met them. I still haven't met them to this day. But I'm going to tell you something through LinkedIn® because of Scott. I was able to connect and close these people.

So, you're sitting on the fence. Time to get off!"

Learn more about Janis at https://jtfitnessandgolf.com/

Key Takeaways:

- Commit to doing something every day to build your network. Do searches on Mondays and Fridays. On Tuesdays,

Wednesdays, Thursdays, Saturdays, and Sundays, send your connection messages via the "my network" area. Respond to incoming messages every day.

- Do specific searches to find people with your shared interest and look for people with few shared connections. This increases the possibility that these people have not heard about your opportunity yet.
- Have a marker so that you can keep track of your recent connections. This will help you not skip any new connections or accidentally send an opening message to the same person more than once.

Chapter Five

How To Start Conversations With New Connections

I've thrown out a lot of information to grasp, so let's recap what we've learned. In chapter two, we went over setting up your profile to make it look the most attractive it can be to your network so that when you're connecting with people, they're thinking, "This is the mirror image of someone that I'm looking for to connect with." You will get a higher percentage rate of people accepting your connections.

In chapter three, we went over a specific technique of looking and searching for the right kind of people for your network whom you may want to network and collaborate with. You don't want just anyone. You want specific people, and we went over how to do that.

In chapter four, we took all those pieces and put them into play in a specific way to connect with people regularly to build a massive network of the right people for your network.

Now we've got all these new connections. What do we do with them?

Great question!

As we went through the connection process in the previous chapter, we are building our network and getting new connections. Now it's time to do the actual work, messaging people. Now that we have all these new leads and connections, we need to do something with them.

There are a couple of different scripts that you can use. One will be an example of a very laid-back, relaxed script, and the other will be a more specific script for the targeted person you're looking for, and you can decipher which one feels better. Then we'll go over the conversion rate of the messages you send people and what kind of responses you can get back from that.

The key to messaging someone on LinkedIn® is to make sure your message is humanizing and genuine. Too many people are getting bombarded daily with automated messages from software attached to their profiles (which goes against the LinkedIn® User Agreement and can get your account suspended if caught) and straight-up slimy sales pitch messages with no human connection being formed. Many users of LinkedIn® are frustrated because they are curious as to why so many people do not respond to them when they do send them a message. As I mentioned, the decreased response to messages is because of the automated and sales pitch messages. The goal is to create and craft an authentic message that resonates with the individual receiving it. Now let's dive into the messaging process.

First, identify to whom you will send a message. Let's say you have someone named Shannon on your list as an example. Next, you're going to click "Message." The first type of message is a very relaxed one, which I am comfortable sending to people because I've worked through different kinds of scripts—with some, I was particular. With others, I was less specific. In this script, I'm about to show you get a very, very high rate of return for someone open to connecting. If this exact verbiage doesn't feel right to you, I want you to make it your own, but use this as a foundation of what you can build from.

Here's what I would say:

"Hi, Shannon. It's great to be connected to you. Do you have any time this week or next week to discuss what we are currently working on and how we can best support one another here on LinkedIn®?"

Edit your message to ensure everything is spelled correctly, copy the message, and send it. Go to the next person on your list and paste the message into the message box. You will change the person's name because this message is going to a new person. Just like that, two messages were sent out. That's how quickly you can go through messaging these people.

Again, that is a very, very simple message, and if that doesn't feel good to you, then do a message that does feel good to you.

Now let me show you an example of the other script I use. Let's use Larry as an example this time. If I was going to message Larry and I wanted to be more specific, here is something that I would say:

"Hi Larry, and it's great to be connected to you. I noticed that we shared a background in XYZ profession/industry, and it would be great to hop on a call to learn more about what we both are doing and how we best support one another here on LinkedIn®. Is there a day and time that works best for you?"

This is much more specific and may feel more comfortable because LinkedIn® is seen as more "professional" than other social media platforms.

Here's how you want to break it down.

"Hi, Larry. And it's great to be connected to you." Obviously, you're edifying the person.

"I noticed that we shared a background in XYZ profession/industry, and it would be great to hop on a call to learn more about what we both are doing and how we best support one another here on LinkedIn®." You're telling Larry exactly why you messaged him with a relatable connecting point, which is good.

"Is there a day and time that works best for you?" Now, this is a crucial line. When you say, "*Is there a day and time that works best for you?*" you're asking a specific question. Specific questions lead to specific answers. If you don't A.S.K, you can't G.E.T. You must ask in order to get.

Again, you can see the difference. There is a more straightforward and specific method; furthermore, it's entirely up to you. There is no right or wrong message to send because you don't know how that person will respond.

What I can tell you is this. I'm always playing around with different scripts and messages to see what will play best on the network I've built.

The other thing that I can tell you is that every response rate is different.

There are three kinds of responses you can expect. There's a 33% chance of getting a response. They're either going to say:

"Yes, let's talk." "No. I'm not interested", or they say nothing at all.

Those are the only things that can happen. There's a 33% chance of people responding to want to hear what you have to say.

I will give you a couple of tips. Some people who say yes might say, *"Yes, but can you be more specific,"* or *"Yes. Can you send me some information?"*

Here are my two tips. When someone says, "Yes, can you be more specific," I would then write back,

> *"Specifically, I want to connect to discuss what we both do professionally and how we can support each other on LinkedIn®. Do you have 10 minutes to talk?"*

For the person who asks, *"Can you send me some information?"* I would write back:

"I would love to send you some information. But before speaking on the phone, I'm unsure what information is best to send. Do you have 10 minutes?"

The other thing that you need to think about is if you're going back and forth with someone via email or messenger, you can't get them on the phone, and they're unwilling to set up a phone call, you must ask yourself, "Is this person the type of person I want to connect and network with?" Chances are no because, in any business that's grown online or offline, it's driven by conversation, it's driven by phone calls or Zoom sessions. If these people are unwilling to do that and want to hide behind their email, they're not a good fit for your network.

In the next chapter, we'll cover an example phone call, how it goes, what information to send, and what to do if they say yes to your offering, product, or service.

Later, we'll go over what you should be doing in your groups and publishing articles/newsletters so you can bring people in that way and provide engaging content. We'll also go over what you should post on LinkedIn® and what you should not.

We will also discuss other ways to start conversations with people through your posts, happy birthday messages, work anniversaries, or job changes. LinkedIn® gives you built-in opportunities to re-connect, so we will discuss how to utilize those opportunities best.

Success Story:

Corey Baker – Best Selling Author/Speaker/Coach

Our society wants to blame everyone for everything. We blame political parties. We blame our kids. We blame our parents. We blame our bosses. Or the economy. Or our mother-in-law. So much of our life is out of our control. There is one thing we can control. We can control ourselves. We can control whether we put ourselves on a path towards becoming the best "us" we can be.

All of us have a person that we long to be. That person is fit. That person doesn't get impatient in traffic. They are generous and forgiving, and bold. The problem for many of us is that the person we currently are and the person we long to be often have a gap. ***Chasing Better*** *was written to help you close that gap.*

In Chasing Better, Corey will talk about some critical areas of your life that you are absolutely in control of. You will laugh. You will be inspired. You will identify a few areas of your life that you can Chase Better and begin the process of becoming the you that you have always wanted to be.

Chasing better is introducing you to the person you have always longed to be. Each of us has a "me" that we want to be. The problem for many of us is that there is usually a large gap between the person we are and the person we long to be. Chasing better is about helping you shorten that gap. Written in an inspiring, honest, and humorous way, author Corey Baker shares from his personal experience how he has "chased better" in many areas of his own life. As a former minister, Corey has dealt with his fair share of personal challenges.

While Chasing Better wouldn't be classified as a Christian book, Corey uses past church experiences to help readers identify areas to improve in their everyday life. Everyone that reads chasing better will be able to identify with one of the critical topics that Corey discusses. Topics in the book include Fear Overcoming being worried about what others think about you Importance of coaching, Reading and journaling, Health Money, Communication Encouragement, Empathy Listening, Learning to love what you do, and Getting better at things you are bad at. Chasing better is an equal mix of easy read and in-your-face challenges. It will encourage you. It will inspire you. It will make you laugh. It may make you angry at times. It will make you a better person and help you become the person you have always longed to be.

Corey is a husband, father, coach, author, speaker, and avid

Chicago Cubs fan. His life's passion is to help people become the best version of themselves. Having spent two decades in full-time ministry, Corey now works from home and lives with his family in Lexington, Kentucky. Corey loves to write and communicate with an equal balance of humor and candor.

"My name is Corey Baker, and I am a health coach and best-selling author, and run an online business and have built our business almost exclusively utilizing Facebook® and a little bit of Instagram®. But to be honest, I was a tad bit intimidated by LinkedIn® and just not quite sure if it was a good fit for us in our industry.

But I will tell you that I have started utilizing Scott's methods by reading this book, then began some consultation stuff, and have since hired him to coach my wife and me on LinkedIn®. And I cannot stop having conversations, meetings, and opportunities for referrals utilizing his methods to crush LinkedIn®.

So, I just cannot recommend him highly enough to assist you in growing your business if you're looking to create more revenue and more influence within your business that you're creating".

Learn more about Corey at https://coreybaker.us/

Key Takeaways:

- Use the template messages I provided or adapt them to your needs. Your messages to your connections need to feel authentic and comfortable for you.
- How people respond to your messages could be a clue as to whether they are a good fit for your business or network. You don't need or want to work and connect with everyone.
- There are only three ways someone can respond to your messages: Yes, no, or nothing at all. If someone wants more information first, you can still get them on a call with the script provided in this chapter.

Chapter Six

You Have Someone On the Phone, Now What?

Now that we have some calls set up let's talk about what we will say to them. Getting someone on the phone is one thing. Still, you can make or break the relationship immediately if you don't know how to present yourself and what you could offer the individual in your service or a collaboration.

With that in mind, let's discuss what I say to people every single time once I get them on the phone.

I'm going to demonstrate a best-case scenario. Of course, there are going to be some things that come up, and not every conversation will go exactly as planned; that's just the nature of the beast. If you stick to the process and do things as I do, you will have better quality connections, collaboration opportunities, and more sales in your business. You will have more genuine conversations, making more people open to your offer.

So, let's jump right in.

For example, let's say we will be speaking to Dominic today.

Dominic and I have been messaging back and forth. We finally set up a call, and he's interested in connecting more. To prepare for the call, I constantly review someone's profile first and look it over so I can learn more about what they do. Let's say he has a background in business coaching, podcasting, and public speaking, which is great because I have that same background. As I look through a profile, I always endorse the person to show that I've taken a genuine interest in who they are before I get them on the call. When I have a call set up, I usually use Zoom, Skype, or my phone. Let's say that Dominic is from the U.K., so I typically would be doing the call on Zoom or Skype. If you have an international calling plan through your phone or have WhatsApp, then, of course, that's an option. The best way to do these calls is through video, if possible. There's nothing like being able to see who you are talking to and being able to read body language. You can connect on more levels than through a regular phone call.

Here's how I would structure my phone call.

I would start this way:

"Hey, Dominic, Scott Aaron from LinkedIn®. Thank you again so much for taking the time out to speak today. I can see that you also have a background in podcasting, business coaching, and public speaking. Tell me a little about yourself and where you see yourself and your business in the next 3-5 years?"

What I've done is that within 30 seconds, I've put the conversation with that person. The reason why you do that is that people like to hear themselves talk, plain and simple. The more someone can share something about themselves, the more they will lower their walls with you. Just remember, we have two ears and one mouth for a reason. Get the other person talking and listen to what they are saying. The best way to stay engaged in the conversation is to get a little piece of paper. People will sometimes unconsciously complain about things they're unhappy with or do not like about where they are in life and business.

I always make notes about those things so I can wrap my personal story around those same things. The goal is to be relatable, so listening, acknowledging, and sharing my own stories around those same things will increase the connection between us. You want to raise the camaraderie level and lower the resistance wall. I let people talk so I can learn as much as possible.

While Dominic is talking, he is probably talking about his life, what he's doing, and what he likes and doesn't like. When he is done, I say:

"Dominic, thank you for being transparent and sharing your story with me. Would you be interested in learning about me, my story, and what I am working on?"

At this point in the conversation, you want to move to all "yes or no " questions because you want to be very clear about where the conversation can go. If he says "yes" and stays engaged in the discussion, you are still in the ball game. However, if he starts saying "no " and begins acting disinterested, that's a sign that you should probably end the call sooner than later. You don't want to waste each other's time.

You might continue by asking:

"Great, Dominic. Is it okay if I share my story with you?"

Chances are pretty good that he will say "yes" to this.

Then you would say:

"Awesome. So, Dominic, I can relate to what you said. I can relate to some of the same struggles you're going through right now. I've been a business coach and podcaster for years, and I've put in over 60,000 + hours in the industry. But some of my greatest frustrations came from the fact that I only got paid when I was closing one-on-one coaching clients. I wasn't getting paid if I wasn't picking up a client. If I went on vacation, I wasn't getting paid. And I think my biggest fear, Dominic, was that if I got sick or had to take significant time off, God forbid, I would be cut off from my income. There was no Plan B. I only had one plan, and it was Plan A. Becoming a father shifted

things for me because I knew the importance of having other means of income behind what I was doing."

"So, all of that, plus all the hours I was coaching, had me not feeling good about the road I was on. I constantly had to sell and wasn't creating meaningful connections. Sure, I was closing sales, but I still had just an active income stream versus a passive one. That led me to think about other ways to create more income with what I taught in my one-on-one coaching. So, eight years ago, that led me to create a virtual coaching course that could be bought at any time, by any person, and it didn't require me to fill up my calendar with hours and hours of coaching sessions."

This is where you would talk about how you created your program or course. When I mention the process of what I did to create it, I would say, "Dominic, have you ever thought about creating a course or program based on what you teach in your one-on-one coaching?"

In this example, most people you're talking to will give you one of two different responses.

"Yes, I do, and it's going great," or "No, I don't but always thought about it."

If they already have a program or course they are offering, you can simply move to close the conversation by asking, "With what we both are doing, how do you feel we can best support each other's businesses?"

We all know how to work our way around that. You'll hear the two most common answers: "*Yes, but I don't know too much about it" or "No."* Those answers are the same because if they don't know too much about it, they don't know ANYTHING about it.

If the answer is "No, I don't have an offering outside of my one-on-one coaching," I would move the conversation to my passion for what I do.

Dominic, that's my story, but it's not my passion. My passion is showing other coaches like you and me the benefits of having another income stream behind what you're doing based on your one-on-one coaching. Whether it's to replace your income made in your coaching sessions, add to your current income, or add a way to create income where you are not trading time for dollars—whatever it is—there is a way to create just that. Now my a-ha moment came about when I was taking a vacation with my family because you and I both know time off is a week of no money because we aren't closing sales—but this week was different."

So that Saturday that I was on vacation, I got a notification in my email that I had ten people purchase my $1000 course that day. Now comparatively speaking, that's not what I would have made if it had been my one-on-one coaching, but at that point, it was the first time in my career that I ever made $1 not having to get on a call to close a sale. That was my a-ha moment. Dominic, would you like to learn more about this and how I help others do the same?"

At this point in the conversation, he's either running for the door or crawling through the phone/computer because he wants to learn more, because every person you're talking to in your network that has a similar background as you doesn't have what you have, wants to create that extra stream of income sitting on the beach, and it's real. So, we're going to go with the best-case scenario and assume Dominic says, "Yes, let's set up a time to talk further about this."

Here is how you then book the call:

"Awesome, so Dominic, here's what I want to do. I want to send you some specific information about my programs, how they are structured, and how I help others create programs that

sell passively. That way, you can wrap your arms fully around this, you can write down any questions you have, and we can set up a follow-up call for two or three days from now. I can answer those questions, and if you would like to move forward, I can tell you what the next steps would look like. How does that sound?"

He then responds with a date and time that works for you, and you close it out with this:

"Great. Dominic, what's the best email to reach you at? Awesome, and how is Friday, a couple of days from now, at 3 o'clock? Perfect, you're in the book. Dominic, I'll send that information out shortly, and I look forward to following up with you on Friday. Have a great day."

Click (hang up the phone)

Now you can choose to send whatever information you want. I typically send things about my products, my business structure, and something that will give them a good picture of this.

Now here are the raw numbers. With any person you can get to a follow-up looking at your information, you have a 25% chance of closing that person because you'll get them back on the phone. They're going to say, *"Yes, let's do this." "No, it's not for me." "Not the right time. Can we reschedule for about a month or two from now?"* Or they don't show up at all, which happens all the time. Now the best-case scenario is if someone says, *"Yes, let's do this, let's move forward, Scott."* You then go over the different offerings you have and which ones are best for that individual.

Here's how you handle that.

"Dominic, that's great. With the information I have provided, are any of my program options the best fit for you and what you are looking to achieve with your business?"

Asking that question will have your connection tell you which program you'll close them into, and then you coach them just like any other client you have worked with.

It would help if you now understood how you have a conversation with someone who agreed to speak with you about your products, goods, or services. Review this chapter as many times as necessary. It will take practice to get used to answering questions and compellingly telling your story. Remember what T.Harv Eker says, "Every master was once a disaster."

Use my scripts as a guide and adapt them to your use. You want to assess how interested someone is in hearing more and create curiosity through your own story. What was your life like before your business, what have you gotten out of it, and how has your life changed? Notice that I did not make any outrageous claims in my story. I didn't promise anyone they would make thousands of dollars right out of the gate, and you can't make guarantees. You have no idea how much someone will apply themselves once they join your programs. Review my story to guide you.

In the next chapter, we'll go through the basic LinkedIn® posting system of how you can start providing some content to draw even more people into what you're doing so you're not spamming; you're simply connecting and messaging.

SUCCESS STORY:

Gary J.Miles, Esq – Podcaster and Top Business Coach To Law Professionals

Gary helps you ***uncover those hurdles*** *holding you back, identify them, ascertain their source, and most importantly, give you actionable steps you can apply daily to* ***free yourself from those prisons*** *that entrap you.*

Gary tailors his unique coaching sessions to ***focus entirely on your specific concerns****. He does not use a "cookie-cutter one size fits* *all approach."* ***Your needs matter to Gary!***

He will meet virtually in one-hour sessions to identify your concerns and fashion a solution with you.

Gary brings over four decades of experience as a problem solver to his coaching business. He is passionate about helping his clients discover the blocks holding them back and freeing them to achieve their dreams better. He has helped clients and parties resolve thousands of issues and disputes over the years. He is blessed with a calm demeanor and is an empathetic listener.

Those who have worked with him find him inspiring, motivational, wise, patient, thoughtful, and an exceptional listener. He has used those skills to coach many attorneys, entrepreneurs, and other professionals to achieve their goals and enjoy a fulfilling life they did not think possible.

Gary is passionate about healthy nutrition. He believes clean nutrition fuels our body, creates mental clarity, builds better sleep habits, and gives us more energy. Although not a nutrition expert, he has successfully coached clients about clean nutrition habits.

Gary Miles has been a high-level trial attorney for over 40 years in various areas, including transportation law, serious personal injury, family law, and estate disputes. He presently focuses on family law and loves to lift and support his clients when they are in a tough place.

He has been the managing partner of Huesman, Jones, and Miles for over three decades. He has been an active member of many professional associations, including the American Bar Association.

He is a trained mediator with over 120 hours of mediation training. He has participated in over 1000 mediations and settlement conferences as counsel for one of the parties and as the facilitator. His studies featured specialized training for divorce mediation, including a focused course on child access, property and financial issues, and commercial litigation mediation. He delights in helping clients solve their challenging problems.

Gary is a proud blended family member, with two children (including Buddy, his law partner), three stepchildren, and five grandchildren in a growing family. His wife Brenda is a Director of Nursing. He and Brenda recently relocated to Pinehurst, N.C., where they enjoy the company of their two treasured English Goldens, Ellie and Dezi. They return to Baltimore frequently to visit family and friends. He is very active with his family and enjoys a variety of recreational pursuits, including playing golf and pickleball often, going to the gym, and taking his pups for long walks through the neighborhood.

"My name is Gary miles, and I'm a podcaster, Lawyer, and business coach. Some years back, I was suggested that I read this same book on how to build a business and network through LinkedIn®. I then did a group training with Scott, which whetted my appetite but didn't fully satisfy what I needed. So, I hired Scott as my coach to help grow my business using LinkedIn®. Full transparency, I have not been 100% on point with what he taught me, but with only being 90% daily of following what he suggested to me, the results are somewhat beyond amazing to me. Even somewhat, almost overwhelming.

I am an attorney with my law firm, and I have time I devote to my online coaching business and podcast, but I don't have unlimited time, and this is just incredible to me how effective it has been.

Given where I am in my life and using Scott's system, I've had about 20 Connect calls with new connections per week. I am getting many more followers on LinkedIn®; I'm getting much more engagement, and I have closed new business on LinkedIn®.

I'm averaging four calls a day and a couple on the weekends if I choose to, and I credit that all to Scott's system but the time he has spent coaching me. I highly recommend that any of you genuinely committed to building your business consider hiring Scott as your coach and using his system.

It only works if we work it, and I've learned that, but I'm committed to working it and continuing to work it. I honestly cannot evaluate my future because I can't comprehend the volume of calls and the amount of engagement I've been getting. So, thank you, Scott, and all of you who are reading this; I strongly recommend that you consider it too!"

To learn more about Gary and his services, visit https://www.garymiles.net

Key Takeaways:

- When you get someone on the phone, let them tell their story before you share your opportunity. This enables you to know what to do next.
- The person who is asking the questions controls the conversation. Steer the direction of the call by asking yes/no questions to keep the other person engaged.
- Your prospect will respond one of three ways: Yes, no, or not now. If they say yes right away, give them the appropriate options with the offerings you provide clients.

Chapter Seven

Creating Engaging Posts on LinkedIn®

If all we did was message people and try to get people on the phone, some people might view us as spammers—that's the last thing you want someone to think about you.

People will look at how active you are on LinkedIn®, which means posting relevant, engaging content. This platform rewards you for being more active, so let's discuss best practices for this.

On LinkedIn®, you will want to post a minimum of three days a week (Monday, Wednesday, and Friday), but no more than once per day. I have found that the more relevant the content is, the more of an attractor factor you will have, not only to your network but to the people you're bringing into your network.

Here's what I mean. The "Notifications" section is great because it shows you lots of great information about your connections, such as birthdays, new job notifications, work anniversaries, and engagement statistics for your posts.

Here is an example of a recent post that I made on LinkedIn®:

"My biggest goal professionally for this year is ________!" Having goals is beyond important when striving to achieve bigger and better things in the coming year. Nancy and I set both personal and professional goals each year. We all need a bullseye

to fire at to progress. My question is this.... Do you set professional goals the same way you set personal goals in the new year?"

When you make a post, you want it to be relevant, relatable, and accurate. It is essential to set goals each year to ensure you are striving toward what you want to accomplish. This post showed a side of me that humanizes me to my audience. You want your audience to feel connected to you and the content that you produce. I want to point out one more essential thing. Being relatable does NOT mean sharing your trash and letting it sit there.

Many people use social media to complain about their lives, but I believe that if you share something important, you should also share a resolution. Your entire focus should be that you are someone who can solve a problem—that's what your business does. You want to have the reputation of being a problem-solver, so all your posts—whether it relates specifically to your business or not—should reflect that.

This specific post had some activity, so in the Notifications, I can click on the activity associated with that post and see who's engaging with it. This allows you to stay in good contact with your network. You can see which specific people are liking and commenting on your posts, so I can like and reply just to stay in touch.

Another thing you can do is go through everyone that likes it and send them a nice little message. So, if Steve, for example, liked my post, I can shoot him a message and just say, "Thank you so much for liking and supporting my post."

This does one of two things: it will lead to nothing where he doesn't respond, or it might lead to something where he might say, "You're welcome." And if he says you're welcome, then this is where you can open a conversation just like we discussed previously, *"You are so welcome. I know we haven't spoken before, but would you have some time to hop on a call or zoom to see how we can support one another here on LinkedIn®?"* Use whatever script you want to use.

If the door of conversation is open by reaching out, and they reach back, you can do whatever you want. When that door swings open, I pounce all over it with a genuine response. This is another way to stay engaged with your network and generate more sales for your business.

The other thing I like to do is look at the post's analytics. Let's say my post already had 21 likes and 2000 views in the first few hours. My network is around 28,000 connections, so if we break this down, 2000 views would be just over 8.5% of my network. That's not bad for just a few hours.

The great thing about analytics is that I can also see where my views come from. I can click on "View Post Analytics." In this case, I would be able to see that a small portion of those views come from first connections, which are the people I am already connected to, and the more significant amount of those views came from the people I am not connected to yet.

It also gives you the people, what companies they're from, what job titles they have, and the audience areas. This is important for one reason. If there is an opportunity for you to connect with a specific company or job title, you can do a new search for the potential connections within the analytics you are looking at.

Let's say a bunch of those views from my post happened in New York City. I can search for "podcast host," click on "People," then click on 2nd connections to filter out the people I'm already connected to. I will then click on the "locations and" filter by Greater New York City Area because I saw that this was one of my posts' most extensively viewed areas.

Now, this is going to shrink down the number of results that I get. As mentioned before, I look for people with few common connections to me because I am looking for people whom others have not overly messaged on LinkedIn®. I try to keep it to 50 connections or under, as I have previously mentioned. Then I send invitations to all these people.

While trying to connect, you may see people you have previously attempted to communicate with but didn't respond. You may have tried to connect a few months before, but they were legitimately busy and didn't get around to answering you. You could simply write to this person again and ask, *"Would you be open to having a conversation to talk about what we both do and how we can support one another here on LinkedIn®?"*

It's worth one more attempt. Why not try again? You have nothing to lose. They will either say yes, no or ignore you. We already discussed handling that so you could review that information again if needed.

Making the right types of posts is very important. Equally important is seeing what other people are posting. I tend to post educational and informational things, so I also like noticing other people who post these things.

You don't always want to be making sales-related posts about your business. People don't care until they know you but will never buy anything from anyone they don't "know, like, or trust." Putting your ego aside will probably be the smartest thing you as a human can do. That's going to get good engagement because it's very value-added.

One type of post that I do weekly is a "LinkedIn® Poll" question. I love polls because they allow me to find out what my target market and clients are struggling with or a pain point they may have in business. A prime example is when I asked my audience, "What are you struggling with most on LinkedIn®?" What this did for me were two things. First, after the poll closed a week later, it gave me a peek into what my network was struggling most with so I could better understand where their pain points are. Second, it allows me to create content based on my network's struggle and provide a solution in the form of another post.

Another example of a successful post I made was a video I did entitled:

"Four benefits to producing video content on LinkedIn®."

Below is what I said in the video but what I also included in the text body of that post:

"First, people cannot only see you, but they can also feel your passion. Think about how many written posts are produced on LinkedIn® each day. Think about how many people scroll past each one because they all end up blending together. When someone comes across a video, it causes them to stop, pause, and listen to what the person says. When someone can feel your passion, hear your passion, and see your passion, it will help you stand out in the crowded space of content on LinkedIn®.

Second, it builds credibility faster with your audience. Again, we are always looking to generate new ways of building credibility with our audiences on LinkedIn®. Video enables us to do that much more streamlined and quicker. When you commit to creating consistent video commentary on the topic or subject you know best, you are genuinely and authentically seen as the expert in your space, thus creating instant credibility.

Third. the "know, like, and trust" is communicated much easier via video. No one buys anything or invests in anyone they don't "know, like, or trust." Video content is a beautiful and easy way to build that trust with your audience over time. When someone can easily relate to you, and you are doing your part in providing solutions to their problems, when the time comes for someone to pull the trigger to invest, guess whose door they will come knocking on?

Lastly, it makes you stand out from others in your space. We must do whatever we can to stand out in the crowded and saturated world of online marketing. Video content is consistently considered one of the best ways to stand out in a crowded marketplace. Yet so many are not taking advantage of it. Why? The long and the short answer is FEAR. We end up standing in our ways of engaging, inspiring, and encouraging those around us to do and be better. The fear will subside when you realize how impactful video can and will be for your business".

One common question I get is, "Are there good times to post on LinkedIn®?" In my experience, there is no perfect time, but if I were to give people a specific time to post on LinkedIn®, I would say between 7 am, and 9 am EST would be best.

This time would be best because global individuals on LinkedIn® tend to most commonly be active before they leave for work, on a lunch break, and after their kids (if they have them) go to bed. Because LinkedIn® is highly global, when you post in the AM, you can have your content more readily visible that way.

Another example of a great post is something that is a tip or "list type" post. I like doing these posts because "how-to or list posts" get 3x more engagement than a regular inspirational post. Giving a simple solution-type post can build trust, rapport, and a significant connection with your audience. It doesn't have to be anything too deep. A simple post about "4 tips on how to create work-life balance" would be highly value-added to your network.

If you have not made a post on LinkedIn® before, click the "Home" icon at the top of the page. Then at the top of your home page, you will see where you can make a post. Click the "Images" icon (it has a camera next to it), and you can access photos from your computer or device and upload them to your LinkedIn® post if you choose.

I find that it's best if the post is relevant to people in my network and aligned with my mission to inspire people to live the best life possible. An example of this for me would be the following:

"It's never about being the best. It's all about being your best."

The idea is to put content out there that engages your audience. That lets you start conversations because it's not about connecting and messaging. You must provide content that will enable people to want to talk with you.

Once again, messaging people and thanking them for liking and commenting is a great way to stay connected to people in your network. Providing valuable and relevant content will encourage them to engage. To me, it doesn't matter whether they are liking or commenting. I see them both equally because they have taken action to appreciate your posts, so I appreciate them in return with messages. If it leads to further conversation, it's even better.

To summarize, you want to post relevant three times a week at a minimum. Remember, the more value-added the content is, the more connection you will build with your network.

That's it.

People will respond most to very relatable things. That means sharing not only positive, educational, and motivational things but sharing things about your business.

For example, I previously finished self-publishing my first book. That is very relatable to people because so many aspire to do that, or perhaps they already have. That post got 141 likes and 25 comments, but most importantly, it got almost 8,100 views from my 25,000 connections.

You always want to look at the views because you want to see what networks they're coming from, job positions, job titles, and locations, so that can help you with your searches.

That is the benefit of posting on LinkedIn®.

In the next chapter, we will dive into things you can do in groups, why you join them, what things you should do weekly, and publishing articles that are creating your blog posts on LinkedIn.

SUCCESS STORY:

Cyndi Walter – Online Wellness Business Owner

Five years after starting my independent home-based health and wellness company, a film crew was sent to my home to produce a successful video about my business.

I guess it is cool that a stay-at-home mom from a rural area in Amish Country could build a dynamic organization and create so many leaders.

This is how I see it:

- *God has blessed me with the gift of encouragement.*
- *I feel led to serve others in all areas but especially their health.*
- *I want to make a difference in this world and impact other people.*
- *I want to be a role model to my family, friends, and associates and equip them so they too can impact others.*
- *I want to teach people how to do what I have done.*
- *I get to love on people all day long.*

My job is to expand our organization of dedicated and supportive people seeking wellness and mindset solutions to discover a better version of themselves. I consider it a HUGE honor to help every single customer. My blessing is that none of this feels like work because I am fulfilled and doing what I am called to do. If you are ready for a change, looking for more fulfillment, or simply prepared to feel better…you owe it to yourself.

Before her current company, Cyndi built a profitable business with two direct selling companies, but she never fully reached the success she knew was possible. Cyndi loved her business and was at the top level for six years, but when there was no longer an opportunity for growth, she decided it was time to move on.

"I loved it there; I had started to save some money, I had the opportunity to travel, and I got into personal growth and development," remembers Cyndi, "but when my income started going in the opposite direction of what I wanted, I knew it was time for a change."

As a marathon runner and fitness instructor, Cyndi has always been passionate about fitness and working out, so she decided to find a company that shared her love for health and wellness. In her research, she discovered Isagenix.

"I couldn't find a product line I liked any better," she says. "The quality of the products and the integrity of the leadership and the Isagenix Team Compensation Plan, I'd never seen anything like it."

When Cyndi first started, she admits it was intimidating and challenging to leave her last business and begin again with her new opportunity. She didn't know much about online marketing and hated leaving her old organization and many friends. She wasn't sure how long it would take to reach the same level of income that she was making with her last opportunity. Cyndi understood that Isagenix was an opportunity she couldn't pass up, and with her husband's support, she got to work.

"I'm Cindy Walter, and I'm in the online business space in the online marketing arena. I hired Scott to coach and teach me how to use LinkedIn® to grow my network and connect with people. He was instrumental in everything from helping me with my profile to learning how to message people properly, doing discovery calls, and following up. It's resulted in growing my business and helping me take it to the next level.

I highly recommend him because, as far as a coach goes, he helps you every step of the way. Still, to this day, when I have questions and need his help, he makes himself available to me, which I appreciate. He's helped so many of my team as well. So, if you're thinking about utilizing him, I highly recommend getting this book and coaching with him because he can help you understand LinkedIn® and use it.

After all, it's a beautiful platform".

Find out more about Cyndi at https://cyndiwalter.com/

Key Takeaways

- When you make a post, you want it to be relevant, relatable, and authentic. Make it something that your ideal audience is likely to resonate with.
- Ideally, you should strive to post 3x per week up to once daily to stay in mind with your audience. You are in the business of solving problems for people, so let your post reflect whether they are specific to your business or not.
- Don't make every post about your business. Being overly sales-oriented is a turnoff. I like to post educational material to engage my audience; then, I acknowledge likes and comments with private messages. These can be conversation starters, just like your daily searches and messages strive to do.

Chapter Eight

Publishing Articles/Newsletters And Using Group Discussions

In the previous two chapters, we discussed the example phone call and how that should lead to the follow-up conversation. Then we went over the posting system, specifically, what you should post, how to look over the analytics, and how to decide what kind of content you should put out there to ensure that your posting is relevant information for your network.

In this chapter, we will go over two other essential components. One is publishing articles/newsletters, and two is starting discussions in the groups you chose to join.

People frequently ask me, "How often should I publish an article/newsletter on LinkedIn®?" The critical aspect of this is to be consistent. I prefer posting one article/newsletter per week. I want to clarify that publishing an article/newsletter differs from making a simple post, as we discussed previously.

You can publish articles/newsletters through a feature called LinkedIn® Publisher, a blog section within your own LinkedIn® account. For example, if I go to My Profile, under the recent activity, it will break down my posts into general posts or articles. I've written close to 600 articles. If I click on this, it will bring up all the articles I have written. Every article I write is based on business tips, business information, and ways to best use LinkedIn® to grow your business.

These are things that everyone in my network can relate to.

I suggest you do the same.

Let's walk through how to do this. Make sure you are on your "Home" page; it will say "Home" at the top. One of the options is to "Write an Article." When you click on that, it will take you to LinkedIn® Publishing. Towards the end of 2021, LinkedIn® introduced a "LinkedIn® Newsletters" feature. It is a feature that is slowly rolling out to the entire LinkedIn community of LinkedIn®, so when you click "Write an article" and don't see the "start a newsletter" feature yet, don't be alarmed. The more consistent you are, the more likely you will be allowed to start your own LinkedIn® Newsletter. My newsletter is called "LinkedIn® Tips and Updates." I started it in November 2021, and I had over 4,000 subscribers within four weeks. When you consistently create an article/newsletter weekly, you will see that kind of growth yourself.

When the blank template comes up for your article, you're going to upload a background photo that directly relates to what you are speaking on (I used Canva to create a background banner that I use for each newsletter for brand recognition), a heading that describes what it is that you are talking about, and then some content.

The photo you use can be something you have saved; the content might be something you have written elsewhere or something brand new. First, find a photo representing what you want to write about or use the template you created on Canva.

One post I made had to do with a LinkedIn® video (I mentioned this earlier in the book) that my audience loved. I believe in working smarter and not harder, so I took the original post and added extra value to it to make it a full-length article/newsletter. As I mentioned, you will want to create an attention-grabbing headline. Boring headlines are unforgivable because people won't read the rest of your article. An example of this could be

"The Most Important Reasons Why You Should Create Videos on LinkedIn®." It inspires curiosity, and that's what you want a headline to accomplish.

Once you have a headline, then you create your content. In this post, I started with a brief introduction of what I would speak about. You don't have to start that way, but it's a great way to get at the main point of your article.

Here is the rest of the content I wrote for this:

"Because there are so many features to use on LinkedIn®, it can distract users of the platform in deciding which to take advantage of. In my opinion, not only on LinkedIn® but on social media in general, video remains the #1 way to connect with your audience to build the "know, like and trust" with them. What people still struggle with regarding LinkedIn® videos is how even to get started. So, what I wanted to first go over is the simple setup for producing LinkedIn videos, whether they are live or native (pre-recorded)

Step 1: Make sure your video is between 2 and 4 minutes long. This will give you and your audience the optimal time to get to know you, but it will give you the time required to deliver the information you are providing.

Step 2: Make sure your video does one of two things. Your video must educate and inform your target audience about what they need to know. Still, more importantly, your video should solve a problem your ideal client is currently having. If you want to be seen as the expert authority in your space, showcase the knowledge that you have regarding your industry.

Step 3: After your video is done and recorded, as you upload it onto LinkedIn®, make sure you write and clear and straightforward description of what the video is about, some bullet points of what you are going to go over, and a simple call to action to engage your viewers.

Step 4: Commit to doing at least 1-2 videos per week. I suggest doing a video on Monday and Friday, this way, you start and end your week with a great visual and audio representation of your craft and skillset.

Now that you have the outline and structure for producing a LinkedIn® video Let's go over the benefits of being consistent with making LinkedIn® videos.

Here are the four benefits of taking advantage of LinkedIn® Video:

1. *People cannot only see you, but they can also feel your passion:*

   Think about how many written posts are produced on LinkedIn® each day. Think about how many people scroll past each one because they all end up blending together. When someone comes across a video, it causes them to stop, pause, and listen to what the person says. When someone can feel your passion, hear your passion, and see your passion, it will help you stand out in the crowded space of content on LinkedIn®.

2. *It builds credibility faster with your audience:*

   Again, we are always looking to generate new ways of building credibility with our audiences on LinkedIn®. Video enables us to do that much more streamlined and quicker. When you commit to creating consistent video commentary on the topic or subject you know best, you are genuinely and authentically seen as the expert in your space, thus creating instant credibility.

3. *The "know, like, and trust" is communicated much easier via video:*

   No one buys anything or invests in anyone they don't "know, like, or trust." Video content is a wonderful and easy way to build that trust with your audience over time. When someone can easily relate to you, and you are doing your part in providing solutions to their problems, when the time comes for someone to pull the trigger to invest, guess whose door they will come 'a knocking' on?

4. *It makes you stand out from others in your space:*

   We must do whatever we can to stand out in the crowded and saturated world of online marketing. Video content is consistently considered one of the best ways to stand out in a crowded marketplace. Yet so many are not taking advantage of it. Why? The long and the short answer is FEAR. We end up standing in our ways of engaging, inspiring, and encouraging those around us to do and be better. The fear will subside when you realize how impactful video can and will be for your business.

   Of the four mentioned, why are you now going to start doing LinkedIn® videos?"

This article expressed what I wanted to say that day, based on the importance of LinkedIn® Videos. Some people post much longer or shorter articles, and there is no set rule about the length of the articles you should write. One guideline I want to mention is to give as much as possible to each article. Give tangible tips, value, site action items, and ways people can improve their life and business just by reading your article/newsletter.

This is something you can do as little as one time per week. Consistency is far more important than frequency. It's better to post consistently once a week than it is to post three times one week than not at all for two weeks after that.

Now that you have finished writing the article, you can also get creative to attract attention to your article by using hashtags that would be relevant to your desired audience. I can type in #linkedin, #linkedintips, #linkedleads (which is my hashtag), #business, and #linkedinvideo — these are all great examples of audiences I want to reach with this.

After you finish, hit the "Publish" button.

Once it publishes, you will be given the option to share it on other social media platforms, such as Twitter® and Facebook®. Doing so will allow you to reach people you are not connected to on LinkedIn®.

Once I share this on my Facebook® timeline, for example, I typically will share this in groups. I will click "Share in A Group," write a little heading and then post it there. The great thing about sharing your article is that this draws people from other social networks into your LinkedIn® network.

At some point, you will want to see how your articles and posts perform, so you will want to know the analytics. You can view your stats by first going to your profile page. Scroll down until you see "Articles & Activity." This should be right above your profile. You can either click to see all articles or see all posts. For example, if you click to see all articles, they will be listed in reverse chronological order. The most recent post will be on top.

You should see the thumbnail of the picture you used for each article, as well as the titles of the articles. It also tells you how many views each article has. If you click on the link to the article, you will see what you have written and how many views, likes, comments, and shares the article has received. The comments will be at the bottom of the article.

If you go back to where the articles are listed in reverse chronological order, you can click on where it shows you the number of views your article had, and it will give you details about who is viewing it. You can see companies, job titles, and locations of the people viewing it. You can also see whether the viewers are primarily first or second connections. If your articles are being reshared on LinkedIn®, there is a high probability that many of your article views will be second connections. This can be valuable information because if your posts are being seen in New York more than anywhere else, you can target your searches geographically when you are looking for new connections, as I discussed previously.

This can be great information for you to use going forward, and it is an activity that can be well worth doing once a week.

Another thing you can do on LinkedIn® is utilize groups. You also want to start discussions in groups once a week.

At the top of the page, you will see a link called "Work." When you click on that, you will see "Groups." When you click on Groups, it will open all your groups. You click on "My Groups," and every single group you belong to is listed on the page for you.

One of the groups I am in is called "The Podcasters Networking Group." If I click on that group, I will see the option to start a conversation. There will be a space to type in a headline for a discussion, then a place to start a discussion.

For example, I love doing pod-swaps (a fancy name for guesting on each other's podcasts). I did a post on the power of guesting on someone else's podcast, so I can copy that post I previously did earlier in the week and then paste it into my LinkedIn® group discussion post.

It's that easy. That can be my entire discussion. Of course, discussions don't have to be posts you have previously done; they can be written discussions based on something new you want to talk about. However, if you have already created content, why not re-purpose it and use it in your groups?

Now, the great thing about a discussion about pod-swapping in a podcaster networking group is that it will draw interest and intrigue, especially considering that there are well over 10,000 people in this group. People might give positive or negative opinions about the topic—it doesn't matter. The goal is to get engagement, not necessarily agreement, although the agreement is excellent if you get it.

You can decide how you want to respond to it, if you do at all, but this is a way to connect with other people to whom you're not connected.

Remember, in groups, you are likely NOT already connected to these people because they are members, not connections.

There is a difference.

The connections are the people that you're connected to. Group members, however, are people likely outside of your regular network. If they engage, if they like, and comment, you can send them a connection and say something like, "Thank you so much for liking and commenting on my post in the group." Treat it the same way you would if someone commented on a post or article you did.

If someone likes or comments on one of your articles, click on the person who commented, then thank them for liking and commenting on your published article. It's all about other ways of starting discussions.

There's something good about this: When people visit your profile, they can see how active you are. They want to see all your activities, including posts, articles, and discussions. They can see everything you are doing and what kind of engagement you are getting.

That's the point. You want people to see that you're not just a spammer.

People want to see that you're providing relevant information and content and things for people to latch onto. Remember that once a week, you want to write an article/newsletter outside the regular posting. Make it engaging, inspirational, or motivating.

No selling. No pitching. No spamming.

Again, make your once-a-week articles about something everyone can latch onto, and then you want to start one discussion weekly in your groups. That will allow you to start meeting more people who want to do something along the lines of what you're doing, grow your network, and impact that network.

In the next chapter, we're going to go over more of the benefits of the Notifications section on your LinkedIn® account and how you can utilize other things that pop up there to start more conversations, have more people get involved in your business, and how you can take that and grow your network even more.

SUCCESS STORY:

Daniel Wright – Online Business Owner and Peak Performance Educator

My Story: I grew up on a small farm in England, driving tractors, milking cows, and making hay. A life that taught me the value of hard work, patience, and satisfaction in the simpler things...I also learned to communicate and build relationships with people from all walks of life. After college and a stint in Industrial roofing, I spent five years in direct B2C sales selling Kirby Vacuum Cleaners door to door culminating in running a distributorship and leading a successful sales team. My wife, children, and I moved to Canada in the late nineties. I spent the next few decades in B2B advertising sales, selling 1000s of ads. And for ten years, I ran a digital marketing agency. Oh, and along the way, I developed a bodyweight fitness course that I taught built on the foundations of what has kept me more robust, fitter, and healthier than men half my age. However, I got tired of the headaches and plate spinning. I realized there had to be a better way to earn a living. After COVID hit, I nearly lost everything and resolved to build a recession-proof and economy-proof repeat income. I did. I found a way to work once and get paid 100 times, creating long-term cash flow. And now, I help burnout 50-year-olds do the same without sacrificing time with their loved ones. Now life is so much simpler and more fulfilling. It can be for you too. I am passionate about helping you realize your dreams. Tangible, significant results in 6-12 months or less.

"Hey Scott, Daniel here. I just wanted to chime in and give you a minor update on how I'm doing with my results, specifically from your coaching. And already, when I started doing the coaching with you, within days, I started getting results.

My Calendar started getting booked up. I have already brought in my first business partner, and my calendar is booked up with quality leads. When I say leads, I'm talking about humans who have agreed to a discovery call with me.

And what's interesting is that I have only implemented probably less than half of what you have taught me. I intend to begin implementing the second half of what you teach beginning next week, and I expect that to accelerate the results I already have. So, I just want to say thank you, Scott, thank you very much for the coaching that you have provided. For me, it's moving the needle. So, I just wanted to chime in, say thank you, and I appreciate all your help, thanks".

**To find out more about Daniel
and what he does, connect with him here:
https://www.linkedin.com/in/danielruperwright/**

Key Takeaways:

- Posting articles/newsletters on LinkedIn® is something you can do as little as once per week. Consistency is far more important than frequency.
- You can also post discussions in the groups you belong to. I recommend doing this once a week also. The idea is to post content relevant to the group, not necessarily about your business.
- When people like or comment on your discussion, you can also send a private message and thank them for engaging. Then you can try to start a conversation just like you would when searching for new connections.

CHAPTER NINE

Leveraging Daily Notifications To Start Conversations

To review what we have done so far, we learned how to reach out to people and schedule calls with follow-ups. We also discussed posting and what to do, how to look to see who's engaging with your posts, and then engaging back. We've also discussed starting group discussions and publishing articles within your news feed.

Let's take another deep look at the "Notification" section on LinkedIn, where you can start to send other messages naturally through ways that LinkedIn® gives you and how those can lead to other conversations.

Every day on LinkedIn®, you will get notifications for anything that happens within your network. This could include someone who likes or comments on a post, someone who viewed your profile, or any activity where there was an interaction with something you did.

There are only four ways that LinkedIn® gets you notified concerning your network.

They are work anniversaries, new job positions, promotions, and birthdays.

This is another excellent opportunity to connect or reconnect with someone in your network because now you can recognize someone for things happening in their lives. In LinkedIn®, there are default messages for all these things: "Happy birthday!", "Congrats on your work anniversary!" and so on.

You can go even further than the automated message provided, and you can customize the message as well. As a result, instead of using only the default "Happy birthday!" message, you can add to it and say, "Happy birthday, Joe. Have an awesome day!" You can add anything to the default message that you like.

The great thing about these notifications is that you now have a chance to recognize someone for an achievement, and it's a warm connection that is being fed to you within your network. You will stand out because not everyone will reach out to those connections and use the push notifications you are being provided with. This means you have a chance to be memorable. You don't want to connect just for the sake of connecting; you want to do it with a purpose.

Essentially, these are simply messages that you have a chance to send to different people in your network every day. As your network grows, you will have more opportunities to reach out to acknowledge these accomplishments.

When you send these messages, there is a chance that someone will reciprocate and say, "Thank you. I appreciate you taking the time to reach out to me."

You'll write a response. Consider this an invitation to begin a conversation, just as you would if you sent messages to your network, as we discussed much earlier.

Use the script we talked about: "You are so welcome. Would you have some time this week or next week to talk about what we both are up to and how we can support one another here on LinkedIn®?"

Don't overcomplicate things. Use the same script you initially created when you were just sending your regular new connection messages. Now you're wrapping that into any way you connect with people on LinkedIn®. Once the door of opportunity is opened, once the conversation has started, you just jump on it. You don't want to miss an opportunity. It's not about being aggressive; it's not about being too pushy. This is about seizing the opportunity to connect with people, and that's the best thing you can do with people.

Every day, you're going to look at your "Notifications" to see who's having work anniversaries, who's celebrating a birthday, and who's changed a job position. These are all additional opportunities to message someone.

Let's say you're organically sending out 5-10 messages a day through the regular new connections that are coming in. Then, between the happy birthdays, the new job positions, and the work anniversaries, that's another 20. That means you're sending 25-30 messages a day. You have a 33% chance of getting a response on those.

Out of 30 messages, you might get between 9 to 12 people saying something back that will lead to conversations.

Let me share an example of what can happen; this is an actual situation that occurred to me with a guy named Larry.

I sent a message, then he said, "Thank you." As a response, I sent him the scripted message.

Then he thanked me for the invitation, and he said that he was not looking for employment.

Next, I wrote, "Hi Larry, I am not seeking to employ anyone. I want to connect with business owners who may need help utilizing LinkedIn® or discuss business collaborations. Is this something you would be interested in talking about?" And he said, "No, I may have a contact that would be interested. Currently, my stepson is in North Alberta working and will be back in Calgary within a week. This may be some of interest to him." And then I said, "Would you be able to pass his info on to me?"

I got his number, so my next step would be to send a message to his stepson.

Asking for referrals from these people (power partners) is also essential. You never know where it can lead.

To summarize, once a day, you'll click on those notifications. You're going to see who is having a work anniversary, having a happy birthday, or celebrating some sort of new job position to drum up more conversations that will lead to more people entering your network.

Now you can piece this all together and start getting the connections and building the network. Have the conversations and move toward converting those into prospects and sales in your organization.

Growing your business organically and naturally is not only possible but very lucrative using LinkedIn® if you do it right.

Most people haven't taken full advantage of the full power of this platform because they simply don't know how.

Now you do. Simply map your plan using the road map provided here, then work on the plan every day. If I can do this, so can you!

SUCCESS STORY:

Dan Kopp – Owner of Dimanico:

Dan is originally from Platteville, WI, and now resides in the Greater Milwaukee/Chicago Area. After high school, he entered the United States Army serving in Frankfurt, Germany, The Republic of Panamá, and Fort Devens, MA. Dan served in leadership roles in the military before transitioning to executive roles within the field of education. Dan has led in various situations utilizing situational leadership while focusing on those he serves. He has mentored and coached executives across school districts and businesses.

Dimanico focuses on three core areas:

Compensation

DinamiComp® is a user-definable, data-driven, parameter-based compensation system in which the organization defines the variables and controls all the limitations.

Coaching

DinamiCoaching™ improves and enhances your leadership skills by focusing on the continuous improvement of your organization.

Consulting:

DinamiConsulting™ provides expert guidance and services in business management, school leadership searches, board development, and data modeling.

"*I am honored to write this recommendation for Scott Aaron. I have only known Scott for about two months, but let me tell you, our interaction has been transformational for me.*

Several months ago, I enrolled in a Mastermind course that led me to understand that I needed to focus on LinkedIn® to interact with my ideal clients. A little research led me to Scott, a guru of leveraging LinkedIn® for business purposes.

When we first interacted, I was lost as a new entrepreneur, having never existed in the business world. I was unsure of my role in my new business and did not know where to start. Scott's impact on me was profound. He allowed me to see the bigger picture of what I was doing and that I had to approach my new role through a networking lens rather than a sales lens.

His tutelage paid off immediately as I could quickly increase my connections with ideal clients, land discovery calls, and expand my presence on LinkedIn® via an orchestrated approach. I am now two months into my new approach, and I am viewed as an expert by those with whom I interact on LinkedIn®.

I strongly recommend you engage with Scott to see what he can do for you. He is personable, professional, and creative and an expert at maximizing the tools available on LinkedIn®".

To find out more about Dan and his company Dinamico, visit: https://dinamicosystems.com/

Key Takeaways:

- Once a day, click on your notifications and send messages to those having a work anniversary, a happy birthday, or celebrating a new job position. It's a great conversation starter.
- If you are sending 5-10 messages a day, then sending 20 messages to those in your notifications, that's 25-30 messages. Chances are, a third of them will respond. Those are great opportunities.
- You can use the default messages to wish people "Happy Birthday" or "Congratulations," but customizing those messages is a better idea because it proves you are trying to engage with people.

Chapter Ten

The Latest Updates To LinkedIn®:

What I love about LinkedIn® is that they are not willing to remain stagnant in the platform's functionality. LinkedIn® consistently looks at what the other platforms are doing regarding communication with one's audience, connection features, and inventive ways of staying in touch with your network.

Since the release of my 1st LinkedIn® book back in 2018, there have been several updates to the platform, and it would only be right to make my latest book as relevant as possible by including every new feature that LinkedIn® has that you may not be taking advantage of, or you may not even know about.

So, buckle up because there are many updates we need to cover. But I can promise you that after reading about how much LinkedIn® has changed for the better, you will never look past LinkedIn® again.

1. The "LinkedIn® Bell:

The LinkedIn® Bell will help you grow your engagement and network organically, and here is how you can do it:

If you check my profile (**https://www.linkedin.com/in/scottaaroncoach/**), you will see that I put a simple call to action in the right corner of my background photo. It says, "Ring my bell to stay up to date on all of my content," with an arrow image directly pointing to the LinkedIn® Bell.

This is something you can easily create on Canva. Make sure there are not too many other words or text to take people away from what action you want them to take, which is to "ring your bell, so your connections are notified of your content updates.

As a reminder, the only people that can ring your bell are those who follow your account or someone who is a connection of yours.

The LinkedIn® Video story feature gives you 30 seconds to clearly state what you do, whom you serve, how you help them, and your different offerings.

Within those 30 seconds, make sure at the end you direct people to go and "ring your bell" to be notified of all your content updates. As a reminder, the LinkedIn® Video Story feature can only be recorded through the mobile app but does appear on the desktop and mobile app.

Again, go to my LinkedIn® profile picture to listen to how I have set mine up.

I have spoken about this before, but you must make sure you are putting a call to action in all the content you produce. If you want people to engage or take a specific action like, "ring your LinkedIn® bell," then you must direct them.

Over time, adding that call to action at the end of your post, adding it to the end of a LinkedIn® Live or native video, or simply just putting in an article or newsletter will boost your total engagement with all the content you are putting out.

2. The "Add to Featured" Option for the "LinkedIn® Featured Content Section:

"LinkedIn® Featured Content" is a section that you can add to "showcase" what you do for a profession, past content that you have posted, or even have calls-to-action to take people from "online to offline" much quicker.

What LinkedIn® is doing now to make it even easier for us to showcase our content is allowing us to add our recent activity directly to our "Featured Content Section."

After you make your post and it goes live, go to that post, and click the three dots on the top right of your content. You will see the option "Feature On Top Of Your Profile." When you click this, it automatically adds this to your "Featured Content Section" on your profile.

If you want to update your "Featured Content Section" manually, head over to your profile and click on "add profile section," then click on "recommended," and it will give you the option of "featured."

You can add your most recent post, article, web link, or even a video source when you click on this.

You can add a link to your calendar, website, or even a direct link to your podcast.

This feature has endless possibilities, and it has helped me and my business immensely.

3. The "LinkedIn® Call To Action Link" Link

A few years back, there was a big problem on LinkedIn®... People were downloading a CSV file of their contacts (email included) and auto-opting those contacts into their funnel. I can't begin to tell you how many lists I ended up on unknowingly.

LinkedIn® caught wind of this and quickly went into action on how they could stop this. They figured it out very fast. GDPR regulations (the rights someone has to opt-in to an email list) were violated by many users of LinkedIn® by downloading and importing their contacts this way.

Because of this, we are no longer able to get access to our connections' emails for such a purpose, which is a good thing. But it brings up a very valid and important question.

How do I get my connections email compliantly and move the relationship from online to offline?

That is a straightforward question to answer...."The LinkedIn® Call To Action Link."

This new feature is being utilized by some and not by many, and I am going over three things you can do with the "call to action link" in your LinkedIn® Profile Headline.

All you have to do is go to your profile, hit the pencil to the right of your name, and when you scroll to the bottom, it will say:

"Website – Add a link that will appear at the top of your profile."

Once you add your link, you can add "Link Text." This lets the visitor of your profile know precisely what they are about to click on or why they should click on the link. This compliantly allows your connections to click your link and opt-in on their own to what you offer.

4. "LinkedIn® Audio Rooms" and they are going to compete with "Clubhouse" directly.

What has me most excited is that LinkedIn® indeed looks at and notices what is going on in the marketplace and what can be improved by bringing it onto its platform.

It's not that LinkedIn® is always "one step ahead"; they do an excellent job of seeing what is created, what is working, and how they can implement it to work even better on LinkedIn.

"LinkedIn® Audio Rooms" is a prime example of this. Now just remember, it is being slowly rolled out, so if you don't have access to it yet, have no fear, as it will be made available to us all soon!

If you are on LinkedIn® to build connection, rapport, trust, and meaningful relationships, this new feature is absolutely for you.

"With the pandemic still disrupting live events and forcing businesses and industry groups to seek alternative means of networking and community connection, LinkedIn® has seen a big rise in live events hosted on its platform, with the creation of Live Events in the app increased by 150%, year-over-year."

– Social Media Today

"First off, LinkedIn® is *launching an initial test of its own, Clubhouse-like audio events platform, enabling users to tune into live discussions in the app and participate by raising their virtual hand to join as a speaker or posting likes in response to the chat.*

LinkedIn® has been developing its live audio tools since March last year, at the peak of the Clubhouse hype cycle. While it has taken some time for the platform to build its own option, it could still serve a valuable purpose within the LinkedIn® environment, providing more capacity for professional connection within industry-aligned meetings and discussions".

– Social Media Today

"We have the professional context to recommend the most relevant events that can help you learn, network, and be successful, and we're investing more in surfacing these events to you. Whether an event by a creator or page you follow or a topic you're passionate about, we will surface the events that will help you reach your career goals."

– LinkedIn®

5. LinkedIn® Video Cover Story:

This is your opportunity to introduce yourself through a 30-second video that you can add to your LinkedIn® profile when someone views it.

It must be uploaded from the mobile app, but it will appear on both the desktop and mobile versions.

This is a game-changer as it allows you to tell the viewer of your profile who you are, what you do, why you do it, and whom you do it for.

The other fantastic thing is that you can update this "cover story" as needed.

If you are changing something within your business or launching a new program, you can edit your cover story to be current and relevant to where you are at that time in your industry.

6. LinkedIn® Creator Mode:

It is so beyond important to "turn on" creator mode. There are two main reasons: First, when you turn it on, it changes the "connect" button to "follow." Why is this important? For those who constantly receive connection requests on LinkedIn® from spammers, this is because they are using software, a VA, or a marketing company to do so. This will block and prevents them from doing so because there is now a 2-step process to send the connection request, as the "follow" button is now present instead of "connect." People can still send you a connection request, but it must be done by hitting "more" under their profile and then hitting connect. If you are tired of getting these, Creator Mode is for you. Second, it also allows you to put what you speak about under your headline. This is key for anyone looking to close sales and pick up new clients. When someone visits your profile, they can immediately see what you speak about; this increases the chances of them staying on your page and following you, which will build the business relationship.

7. LinkedIn® Live Video:

No matter what you may hear, no matter what other experts may say, no matter what other people in your circle may be talking about, video is where it's at.

They may be saying that long-form posting is the way to go. They may say that doing Instagram® reels are the way to go. They may say that doing TikTok® videos are the way to go. Listen, nothing beats going live and creating that connection with your audience, and LinkedIn® Live is one of the best ways to do that.

The crazy thing is that anything you do once that's difficult becomes easier as you go, so in reality, it may be overwhelming to think about going live on LinkedIn®. Yes, it may be a daunting task to go live on LinkedIn®. And yes, it absolutely may feel uncomfortable.

Everything is uncomfortable in the beginning, so what I want to help you understand and what I want to help you move forward with is understanding the 3 top benefits of doing at least 1 LinkedIn® Live video per week.

Something that we are always talking about. We are always looking to achieve credibility and trust with our audiences.

Credibility and trust are built over time, and when you can go live on LinkedIn® and educate and inform your audience on things that they need to know, about what they do for a profession or the industry that they're a part of, people start to look at you with that notion of credibility and being that credible source where they're going to go and get their information.

In addition, when trust is formed and when you have the trust of your audience, a whole new world is opened for you. Going live on LinkedIn just one time per week is going to earn you that credibility, and it's going to earn the trust of your network.

So, they will come back to you repeatedly for more information.

I always tell people to be a "salmon in a world of fish." Go against the grain. Go against the current. Don't go with the flow; go against the flow. Carve your path, blaze your trail.

There are many people in this same space you are in. Whether you're a coach, whether you're a consultant, whether you have a mastermind, whether you're building an online business, there are other people out there just like you.

But what are you doing that's truly different from everyone else? What are you genuinely doing to separate yourself from the other people in your space?

Going Live once a week on LinkedIn® does position you as the expert. You want to be looked at not only as that credible source but as the expert in your space. Now many people consider themselves LinkedIn® experts. Are they? I don't know.

They could be, but whenever I see someone in the space calling themselves a LinkedIn® expert, that is not doing all the things required to be an expert in your space, providing value-added content each day, are they really an expert?

Doing LinkedIn® lives, producing LinkedIn® polls, adding editions to a LinkedIn® newsletter that you've created, and never selling or pitching to your audience about a product, good, or service that you have is what I genuinely feel define someone as an expert.

When they're not doing those things, and when they're giving without expecting anything back in return, while going live once a week on LinkedIn®, where others in your space are not going live, it will position you as the expert in the space.

The absolute truth is that every week without fail, after I produce a LinkedIn® Live, which I now do two times a week, I have someone that reaches out to me to find out how I can help them better utilize and leverage LinkedIn®.

Do you want to know why? Because each week, I hop on LinkedIn® live and provide value-added information and education on things people need to do to move their business forward. If I strike a chord with someone on a specific day where they want to learn how to leverage LinkedIn® to generate a lead, create more conversations, and produce value-added content like I am, they will go to a trusted source.

They will go to a credible source, and they will go to the person who is positioning themselves as the expert in that space. When you go live just once a week on LinkedIn®, you will achieve all those things.

You are going to achieve that credibility. You will gain the trust of the network you're building. You will position yourself as the expert in your respective space, and you will, with all those things aligned in the correct order, generate more leads and sales because of how you are showing up each week on LinkedIn®.

Now that you are fully updated and equipped with all the latest updates to LinkedIn®, it's time for you to put them into practice and crush it!

Every aspect of this book is taken from what I do each day and week on LinkedIn®. From the content to create to the messages to send to how to use the new features. I always practice what I preach and hope you take full advantage of everything that you have learned thus far.

Key Takeaways:

- Take full advantage of what "Creator Mode" gives you
- Live Video is the best kind of video to do on LinkedIn®
- Use these tools to build the "know, like, and trust"

Chapter Eleven

Case Studies, YOU Can Do This.

In this chapter, I will present three case studies of some clients I interviewed. Each of them has excelled in my LinkedIn® Accelerator training program. They all did what I told them to do; they followed the system and quickly experienced results.

I will let each of them tell their stories below.

Case Study #1: Zilah M.

Scott: I finished working with Zilah months back, and she's one of the most outstanding people I've had the opportunity to work with. She got the quickest results out of anyone I've ever worked with.

Zilah took her business to a whole different level. She had 20 calls during her first week of working with me.

Let me tell you a little bit about Zilah first. She graduated from Indiana University. She's a Hoosier at heart and got her MBA from Loyola University in Chicago. If anybody followed the NCAA tournament, they made a fantastic run a few years ago. She was a music teacher for years and then a brand manager, but then combined music and teaching in business. She opened her studio teaching "Mommy and Me" classes. She has been a business owner for ten years and opened her child enrichment center. When her first child was born, she had to take several steps back from working too many crazy long hours.

Today she's a wife and mom of three young children and loves online marketing. This is her first dive-in, and she's only been in it for about four months.

I'll let her tell her story.

Zilah, what about the online marketing business model do you love most? And then the second question, what was it about what you heard on my call that lit a spark for you that you had to do something else?

Zilah: Online marketing is giving me a chance to be a business owner, which is what I love. When I was in business teaching my "Mommy and Me" classes, I would sit down and figure out, "How many classes do I need to teach per day, per week, or per month to make this certain amount of income"?

And my income was capped. There are only 24 hours a day, and kids didn't want to take my music at 11:00 PM. But once I realized my income was limited, I knew that I needed to hire more people because then I could increase my revenue.

But I just kept seeing that no matter what I was doing, how I was putting my business together, or how many kids were in my preschool, there was always a cap.

It wasn't enough. I still poured so much blood, sweat, and tears into this business. I worked so many hours. I enjoyed teaching, but there was stress from not earning what I felt I could or should be earning. So, when I was open to online marketing, I finally had a big a-ha moment—I get it now.

Scott: Let's pause right there. I want you guys to hear what she just said. She had only been doing this for two months and realized that in eight weeks, she had to do more than what everyone else was doing. Most people I work with have been in business for years. They've gone through the trials and tribulations of going through their warm market and spending money on things that just don't work. You saw that within weeks that you knew you needed other things.

So, the second question is, what did you hear me say in the training that made you realize that you needed to learn LinkedIn®?

Zilah: It was about the quality of the people I reached out to. While I love and appreciate my Facebook® friends who have joined me in my business, the people I am meeting on LinkedIn® have different dreams and desires.

I talk to my friends on Facebook® because I want to help them get to the same point I am at—the way I feel physically, mentally, and emotionally. That's what I'm helping and coaching my friends with.

But a friend on LinkedIn® is talking to me because they are also experiencing the same business experiences I've had. They may be working for themselves, or they trade time for money and are looking for another way, and I can say I have another solution. If I can help you add a little more vacation time each year, that would be a huge deal.

Scott: If we break that down, you were connecting to their need. You saw right away that two types of people come into a business. There are the customers who are just happy investing in a product or service that they love. There's no desire or need because the average income of someone on Facebook® is about $30,000 a year, and they're not really on here to build a business. They're here to be social, connect, and show their life, pets, food, family, and everything else.

Then you also saw the need for the other side of online marketing, which is building a team because everyone is so used to pulling down that slot machine—seeing the three cherries pop up and spit out a bonus.

You think, "I'm making money in online marketing!" but that next week, if you don't close a new client, you're not earning because you haven't built the leveraged income side. Remember, a customer or consumer will order when they feel like it. However, when making and expanding a team, you want to spend time on a platform where those opportunities lie.

Zilah: Right. I just sat down with my husband last night, and we figured out where I wanted to be in a year and two years—how many people does that mean—and the magic number that we came up with for me is 2,700 people. I don't know if I can find 2,700 people on Facebook®, but with what you taught me on LinkedIn®, I know that it is beyond possible following your system.

Scott: So, the big question is this. We just did our 6-week training. You started before our first session with the training videos I sent you. Explain how quickly this does happen, just from my step-by-step training videos. We're going to get to the closing of the sales side in a bit as far as getting traction, building your network, and having people willing to get on the phone with you. Paint a realistic picture and tell us how long it took you to implement my strategy to start getting results.

Zilah: Three weeks ago, I listened to the first video on my phone and realized I could do this! I had 109 LinkedIn® contacts in the last ten years of my life. As a result of your training, today, I have 1083 contacts.

Scott: So, you've added almost 1000 contacts.

Zilah: Right, and it's not 1000 random friends. These are targeted. There's a reason for me to talk to them, whether it turns into a business relationship through online marketing or not. I just started reaching out, and the response was tremendous. I'm almost unable to keep up with the response.

Scott: That's more leads than time, which is every business owner's dream. Before you and I spoke, you had between zero and five weekly calls. So, implementing my LinkedIn® strategies, how many calls per week are you having now?

Zilah: I'm probably doing 10 to 20 a day.

Scott: That's an average of 15 calls a day. If you're doing that maybe four days a week, that's around 60 calls. This is normal; this is how LinkedIn® works.

Zilah: I don't even have enough hours to put in all the calls because I have a baby at home. If I am reaching people and have an entire conversation with someone, that means that every 15 minutes, I can schedule a call.

I ask myself, "How can I reach out to all of these people?" My baby must nap, so I'm forced to be at home, and I have reached out on the phone and through the Internet.

Scott: That's the key because I told you that you could have 5,000 friends on Facebook®, but if you have 30,000 friends on LinkedIn®, that's a whole different network of people you're building relationships with.

And again, just so you guys know, Zilah owns a business. She's a wife, and she's a mother of three kids. She has a baby at home. Zilah came to me because she needed efficiency and immediate effectiveness. Zilah, you started getting calls right away. How many days did it take you to get your first sale from what I taught you to see a return on your investment?

Zilah: It was about seven days.

Scott: For anyone out there, if you haven't used LinkedIn® before, your entire business can change quickly if you do this correctly. That new sale could be the diamond in the rough that she would have never been able to connect with if it wasn't for what she's doing on LinkedIn®.

And here's the more significant thing. Zilah didn't want to wait to hit that wall where the warm market started to dry up. She wants to create more leads than time now.

You've gotten phenomenal results. For anyone sitting on the fence and thinking about not just working with me but implementing LinkedIn® strategies—what is the biggest takeaway, you were impacted by concerning what I taught you and what you are implementing into your business?

Zillah: As I mentioned, I'm reaching a different type of person for my business. My closest friends are on Facebook® and Instagram®, and talking about business can get awkward. But on LinkedIn®, business is already the first thing we talk about.

I tell people I have a business and discover if they want to join me. That's a much faster way to get where I'm trying to go. I'm doing everything with integrity, still sharing what I love and having the joy of everything that I'm experiencing.

And Scott, I just want to say I've had a few people reach out to me and ask, "Could you have learned what you're learning on your own instead of hiring a coach? Maybe if I had plenty of hours to fiddle around and research a little bit about how people decide to do things. But I don't have that kind of time to invest in something where there's already an expert, and Scott already knows, and you're going to get it.

Don't spend the next six months researching best practices on LinkedIn®, what you should write, and how the conversations should go. Scotts got it all there for you.

I didn't have to think about what to do; it's done for you. Invest in yourself; invest in the training. All I need to do is close one more sale, and I've just made a return on investment for what I put into myself with LinkedIn®. It's amazing. It's a no-brainer.

Scott: Success leaves clues. I use this example: You go to a restaurant and taste the food and try to figure out the exact ingredients. Then you go home, try to make it, and it comes out completely wrong. Instead, you can just knock on the chef's door and say, "Hey, listen, would you mind sharing the recipe with me? How much would it cost me to learn how to make that right now?"

Last question: How do you feel now about being a professional business owner on the platform of LinkedIn®?

Zilah: For me, this is the dream. I understand how to reach out to somebody from a business perspective, and it feels like I'm making the most of my time. I'm not sitting here waiting for someone to reach out to me on Facebook® and say, "Great, tell me more," and then we go through a series of conversations. This is me getting to take proactive steps toward changing my family's financial future, and that feels good.

I get to make phone calls every day. That doesn't scare me when I say my goal is to have 2,700 people by 2023. But if I had said that before I met you, Scott, I didn't know how I would do that. But now I do.

Scott: Within the first week of working with me, you had an average of 20 to 40 calls a day in your first week and got your first sale within seven days, with more on the way.

This is a game changer. I'm grateful for you and the opportunity to work with you. Thank you for what you're doing, and I already see you are a leader in action. Even though you're only a few weeks in, I can already see your confidence now that you have the tools in your tool belt to continue to be a successful business owner.

Thanks for being here today!

Case Study #2: Luna H.

At the time of this interview, I had known Luna for several months. She had increased her income following my system and looking to go even further.

Scott: Luna, you and I connected several months ago, and you heard me on a call about LinkedIn® lead generation and creating more sales in your business.

So, for people to better understand you and what led you to reach out to me, tell us about your journey before growing your business online using LinkedIn®.

Luna: Absolutely. For those of you who don't know, my name is Luna Hernandez. I'm now a nutritional coach and have a background in nursing. I'm a massage therapist and a personal trainer. I'm also a single mom of a beautiful eight-year-old boy. What led me to want to grow a business using LinkedIn® was that I was tired of being tired like many people are, and I was looking for a solution to feel better. I always felt like a businessperson. I never liked being in a cubicle from nine to five. That was never me. I'm a very creative person, so I did telecommunications for a while. It was the wrong industry for me, and I bombed.

I thought that decision was stupid, so I went back to working a regular job like everyone else. Then in 2017, I got the bug to grow a business online. I just wanted to take back control of my life and time.

Since I had previous experience using the online space to expand a business, I knew my warm market would run out very quickly. I had the advantage that I was a massage therapist, and I would come across people. I was very serious about building income online, but then I plateaued. I didn't know where to go because Facebook® was not giving me any results. Everyone was doing the same thing, and I'm the type of person that says if everyone's going this way, I'm going to go that way instead. I wanted to do something different. I realized that I needed to think outside the box, and that's when I contacted you.

Scott: Thank you for that. I like sharing this analogy with my clients. I teach people to be salmon, not the rest of the fish. All the other fish in the sea swim with the current, but salmon go against the current upstream. What I loved about you when we first connected is that you shared some of the things you were struggling with. I always ask people, "How many conversations are you having daily?" And they say, "Well, not a day. I would say zero to five conversations per WEEK. However, the one thing you and I spoke about is whether you want to trade time for dollars as an in-person contractor or have the flexibility to use LinkedIn® to grow your business online.

So, in our first conversation, Luna, before you said yes to working with me, what were some things you and I talked about that struck a chord with you?

Luna: I had so many a-ha moments that I said, "Why was I never aware of this?" First, I was unaware of the social media change since I last used it to grow a business. It's a massive difference because social media continues to change.

Instagram® and Facebook® are platforms for the attraction market. You're going to have people come to you for products. However, if you're growing a professional business and are serious about it, you need to be more visible on a platform like LinkedIn®.

My issue when I first started was that I was signing up anyone that had a pulse and was breathing. I wasn't qualifying. I just accepted anyone who wanted what I was offering. That's not how to build a good business. You want to work with people who genuinely see the value of what you provide and could most benefit from what you do for a business.

But I didn't know where to find them. What struck a chord was that everything you said was exactly what was happening to me. I wasn't getting serious clients; I was getting people who weren't a good fit for my business.

When you talked about LinkedIn® and the potential of connecting with like-minded people, I didn't know anyone. I'm a single mom, and I didn't know how to find the money to invest in you, but I was going to look for it and find it—and I invested in you not just once but twice because you were that good.

Scott: Thank you. You started to see that there are two sides to this. Some use Facebook® and Instagram® to sell a product. However, at the same time, you have business-minded people spending time on the #1 social media platform for business connecting and networking, LinkedIn®!

It's funny because if you're not getting results from Facebook® or Instagram®, you'll get frustrated. Why wouldn't you want to add something to your plate that will get you results? You realized that if you wanted something to change in your business, you had to change some things you do with your business.

We jumped in right away and started working together. How quickly did you see a return on what I showed you concerning how to use LinkedIn® for building your business?

Luna: I'm going to be raw and honest. I was scared for the first few months because it was something I was not used to. I'm used to people coming to me instead of me going up to people, but I had to get out of my comfort zone. I had just to do those first few calls. Some of them said no, some of them said maybe, and a lot of them were open to the idea. I've been amazed and made some tremendous authentic connections with like-minded people. Every day I'm growing, I'm getting more competent, and I'm talking to people I would usually never talk to if it wasn't for the training you offer.

If you're just on Facebook® and you're saying you're a business owner—news flash, you're not! To be a business professional, you must have many conversations, and I can communicate with 100 people daily on LinkedIn®.

Scott: You said something interesting. You were having a lot of great conversations. Here is one of the most significant differences between Facebook® and LinkedIn®. With Facebook®, you must wait for people to reach out to you when they're ready to talk, but on LinkedIn®, it's the opposite. I showed you how easy it is to connect with the mirror image of yourself and start having conversations.

People always tell me that LinkedIn® isn't their warm market, and they don't know anyone there, so they don't know what to say to them. Let me ask, how easy was it for you to implement the strategy of how I taught you how to reach out to people and have conversations? How open are these people, and how quickly are they responding to you to set up a call?

Luna: It's like night and day, to be honest. On Facebook®, when people are ready, it's okay. You must meet people where they're at, but on LinkedIn®, people mean business. They're in there to network, to collaborate, and they're ready to do business. I message them, I get their number, and we're on the phone, maybe even the same day.

Scott: Before implementing LinkedIn® into your business strategy seven months ago, when you were doing Facebook® and Instagram®, how many total calls per week would you have on average?

Luna: Oh my gosh, maybe four calls a week.

Scott: And how many of those were with unqualified people?

Luna: All of them.

Scott: You're still doing Facebook® and Instagram® because I told you straight up, don't leave those platforms. How many calls do you have per week since implementing LinkedIn® as well?

Luna: About 25.

Scott: So, you've increased the number of calls per week.

Luna: Yeah. Sometimes I would keep going until late at night.

Scott: It's so funny because everyone still uses Facebook® and Instagram®, whether it works or not. When people learn LinkedIn®, they quickly give up if they do not see a return immediately. Let's fast forward from when you started with me to where you are. Share some of the successes that you've had with implementing

LinkedIn® in your business.

Luna: I've gotten in touch with many people in the same industry as me: trainers, registered dietitians, and people who just want to do business with me. They see the opportunity, and the great thing about that is I'm getting someone who falls in love with what I am doing and who needs what I am offering.

Many people need what I have, and the vision of my business is to help as many people as possible. I can run a lot faster carrying a wagon if I have five horses with me than just me pulling everything by myself. That's what LinkedIn® has done for me. It has allowed me to use the power of the internet and connect with people.

Scott: One of my old business coaches, Todd Falcone, taught me something early on. He said, "Instead of dragging the thousands, run with the few," and the few people are the ones that have a great consciousness about money that they're prosperous. They want to do more.

I want to ask you some rapid-fire questions. Have you increased your network since you started implementing LinkedIn®?

Luna: Absolutely.

Scott: Have you increased your sales with all platforms that you're using since you started implementing my LinkedIn® strategy?

Luna: Absolutely, yes.

Scott: Great. Has your business personally grown since implementing LinkedIn®?

Luna: To all of this, yes.

Scott: And most importantly, have you seen a more significant return monetarily into your bank account for all the hard work that you have been doing, implementing LinkedIn® into your business?

Luna: Yes. It's a big difference.

Scott: To summarize, for those who are thinking about

implementing LinkedIn® but they're on the fence about whether it's the investment or the time, what has been the biggest takeaway that you've had? What's the one thing you can leave everybody with to push them over the edge to finally implement this into their business?

Luna: I think they must look at what they're doing and how well that's working for them. Social media is changing, and if you're serious about growing your business, you must start reaching out on different platforms and doing other things. I'm not the most intelligent person, I was an average student all my life, but I'm creative with my ideas.

You need to start being creative. Do things that are different. Look at the types of business owners on LinkedIn®—people with $100,000 or more annual income. They take massive action.

If you're serious about this business—which is what I was—I found the money, I found time, and I just made it happen. Invest in what works. I follow people who leave clues to success.

If you're serious and want to be a professional, go where the professionals are because you're never going to make it just selling to those who aren't qualified with what you are offering. You must be proficient in what you're doing.

Scott: Yes, 100%. So, if you guys are not following Luna on social media, you can follow her at Luna Hernandez on Facebook®, or Luna Hernandez Coach, which is her Facebook® business page. She also has a beautiful website where you can learn more about her other services, and it's www.lunahernandezcoach.com. Again, you want to link arms and connect with the right people.

Again, I want to say that it's an honor and a privilege not only to have you as a client but also to call you a friend and to know that we can bounce ideas off each other. Thank you for your time today sharing your heart, your results, and what you've learned from this.

Luna: Thank you so much. I know in my heart it works. If you're thinking twice about it, I would say just dive in, and I appreciate everything you've done for me. This has helped me grow, and I'm forever grateful.

Scott: Thank you so much for your time here today.

Case Study #3: Kelli C.

I have had the pleasure of working with Kelli, who has tons of experience in the fitness industry. She is the perfect example of someone who knows a lot already and is willing to learn even more because she is humble and coachable.

Here is her story.

Scott: Kelly and I connected on LinkedIn® about six months ago. We both have wellness backgrounds, and I wanted to communicate with her. I knew a bit of her experience, and we talked very quickly and started working together.

I want people to meet the fantastic clients whom I've worked with and have them tell their stories. This time, I have the amazing Kelli Calabrese; she's a 32-year fitness nutrition and lifestyle professional. She's a clinical exercise physiologist with 27 certifications, including medical exercise specialist, clinical exercise, post-rehab, and nutrition. She's owned and operated a chain of health clubs in New Jersey, managed corporate fitness centers for companies like Calvin Klein, and founded a school that prepared over 3000 people to be certified fitness professionals, which means she knows what she's doing. She was the lead fitness expert for E-diets, launched the online training program for fitness, and was the fitness expert for Montel Williams.

So, if anyone knows who Montel Williams is, he was one of the prominent talk show hosts in the late 1990s into the 2000s. Kelly was the international master trainer for Adventure Bootcamp, appeared on all the major networks as a lifestyle expert, and is on a TV show that will launch in the fall for entrepreneurial women. She's also getting ready to launch an APP that will change the country's safety.

So, Kelli, you have a very extensive background, and that's where we connected. I have over 20 years of experience, we've touched many lives, and you are a multiple six-figure income earner in your business.

Many people would say, "Well, Kelli, what kind of help do you need?"

You've written books, appeared on TV and helped Montel Williams. Why would you need to do anything else? You and I both live in the same headspace; as servant leaders, we are always looking to teach and show people how to do more and not to get comfortable where we are always looking to grow.

If someone asks, "Kelli, why did you work with Scott? You're already making a six-figure income. Why Scott, why LinkedIn®, and why his program?"

Kelli: That's a great question. Well, my heart has always been fitness first and to help people be healthy, so it all fits together. I also love that you are a fitness pro and were crushing it using LinkedIn®. There are results and much evidence as to why you are so good at what you teach on LinkedIn®. Why would I not want to find someone more prosperous and just model and duplicate what they do?

I wasn't using LinkedIn®, and even in my mind, I knew it was the professional place to go. I was still doing much hanging out on other social networks.

I just wanted to see what was possible on a more professional level like LinkedIn®, and you had a system that works. I am a system person. If you give me something that works, I've learned enough to duplicate and model someone who's ahead of me and someone who's successful. I wanted to simplify because there's only so much of me to go around.

Scott: Exactly! When we connected, you had 13,000 connections, but you had no idea what to do with them. And I said, "Oh my God. Kelli, you have so much potential here. There's so much room for you to grow.

After our first session, I remember that you texted me and said that you sent 20 messages, and ten people replied and wanted to connect with you—plus, you closed two sales that week, both via LinkedIn®. They were your old neighbors that you reconnected with, but they weren't on Facebook®, and boom—you had ten appointments booked with two sales. You and I are both into simplicity and duplication. We're both into not reinventing the wheel, and let's not change something that's not broken. With those kinds of results, after just one session together, what did that tell you about LinkedIn®, but how powerful is this, and what did it tell you about what I was doing with it?

Kelli: Right. Our first conversation was short. It was maybe 10 or 15 minutes, and I said, "Yes." I knew you had what I needed and made that commitment financially to your coaching. There's no buyer's remorse for me. I knew it was what I needed in the first week. I earned back what I spent on your training.

Scott: That's the idea: learning more to get more back times, however much you invested.

Kelli: Yes, that's correct. That makes things so much easier for them and me because when you get something that works, that's when the breakthrough and momentum happen. That's when lives change—and that's cool.

Scott: What's been the biggest takeaway for you regarding the difference between the caliber of the people that we typically connect with on Facebook® compared to the caliber of people that we now associate with on LinkedIn®? What's been the most significant difference for you?

Kelli: Well, the people on LinkedIn® are professionals, and you could tell right away; they're owners of companies, they're CEOs and high-level management. Money is not going to be an issue for these people. They want to better themselves and their businesses. They're willing to invest in doing that, so the money objection has not been there, which is a beautiful, incredible thing.

Instead, they're saying, "What do I need to do? How can I work with you? Can you help others I know too? That's nice; how much does it cost?" Talking to true professionals is just so much nicer. The income is there. One of the only objections we get is money, which takes that away because they're business professionals.

Scott: The other thing I realized in doing this is that there are many more open people on LinkedIn®. This platform is for networking, and because you and I come from very similar backgrounds, we were so used to waiting for people to reach out to us. But when we are on LinkedIn®, we can simply reach out, have conversations, and book appointments.

Eric Worre said it best: "The scariest aspect about building your business is when you look at your appointment book, and nothing is written down." How much has this helped you, and now helping your team?

Kelli: Oh, it's tremendous. If I open my calendar and there's nothing for the next day, I can spend 30 minutes on LinkedIn® and book up my calendar for the next day, and it doesn't matter what time it is. The beauty of it is that I almost can't keep up, and now that my network is nearly 20,000, I can't keep up with all the opportunities there. If I stopped right now, I would have a lifetime of people to connect with, so I can look at all the people who've messaged me. I send messages to people to wish them "Happy birthday," "Congratulations," or "Happy Anniversary." Then they wrote back, and I took a few minutes to use the most straightforward script you gave me. It is so simple you won't even believe it. It's effortless, and it works.

One more thing: don't change it!

I was tempted to personalize it, but I just do it exactly as you said. Before I know it, people set up appointments with me and hop on the phone. I block 30 minutes times, I can fill my calendar, and I can show it to my team.

Scott: Just to reiterate, when Kelli and I started working together about six months ago, she had 13,000 connections, and she has close to 20,000 now. So, in about six months, she's added 7,000 new connections to her network, which is normal. I went from having 500 connections to just under 25,000; here's a big difference: we're limited to only 5,000 friends on Facebook®, but on LinkedIn®, your limit is 30,000 connections, so you can grow a network six times as large and 20 times as fast.

That's so critical. I teach everyone how to be crab fishermen; if you have seen "The Deadliest Catch, " you're a deep-sea fisherman. You're throwing pods out into the ocean, and then the following day, you circle back around and have crabs in there.

This is the same principle.

As you said, you wake up and have people wanting to talk because the money objection is gone. The average income of someone on LinkedIn® is $100,000 a year. Another big thing is that everyone has an avatar, and there's a demographic that we need to play in. I showed you that the demographic of people on Instagram and Facebook® is 18 to 29—and you and I are not 18 to 29, although we feel that way. Then I expressed to you that the age demographic of someone on LinkedIn® is 30 to 55, which is more of a seasoned professional. You realized that it made sense.

I don't want to say LinkedIn® is not for the faint of heart because it is necessary. You will have a flat-line business for people struggling with booking appointments, having conversations, and closing sales.

What would you say to that person who says, "I need to do something else"? Tell him that he needs to invest in his business. I'm tired of waiting for people to reach out to me. What would you say is the most important thing they should focus on and why? LinkedIn® is an excellent key for them achieving that.

Kelli: One of the cool things with LinkedIn®, as you mentioned, is the search. Let's say you're a musician and want to search for "musicians" in Miami. You can connect with them and create a community. You can build locally to go globally, and there's so much power to that. Perhaps you're in the military and want to connect with military people. For me, it's fitness. I love talking to gym owners, and I know their pain, and I know their hearts. I know what the solution could be for them. You get to talk to people like you whom you want to attract to your business. If you're a mom and you want to talk to other moms who are CEOs, you can search for that in your neighborhood as well. Those are some great examples.

It's not like you've got this list and are unsure what the connection is. You get to search for what you love, choose whom to connect with, and pick specific niches, whether it's martial arts or whatever you are interested in.

Scott: That's the beauty of what you just said. Facebook® and Instagram® are a representation of where you currently live, where you lived, and whom you went to college and high school with. The search feature you mentioned is one of the significant components people forget about LinkedIn®. You can search by city, state, province, and company. Kelli, we were both personal trainers, and there are personal trainers all over the world—in the UK, Australia, New Zealand, Ireland, Spain, and wherever we are, there are people like us. But for you to connect with those people, you need an international social media platform like LinkedIn®.

I always like bringing people successful people like Kelli so you can hear it from them directly.

You have multiple six-figure businesses. You're getting personal results with this. It led to sales in my first week of showing you what to do.

If you could break down and summarize one key that you have

taken away from LinkedIn® that has been an essential tool in your tool belt now, and why everyone else should use that as well, what would that be?

Kelli: It's to follow precisely what you say, Scott. We did a call about the profile. Then we had a call about what it looks like when you connect and how specifically you connect. Then we had a call about identifying your network and how you use messaging. You gave the exact formula. If you just follow it, don't try, and change it. Don't get creative. Just follow what he says.

I'll be honest, I first asked myself, "Is this a business I want to be in? Do I want to log on and wish these people happy birthday, and is this fun for me?"

But when you start seeing the connection, feel the energy coming in, and people are thanking you—it's so worth it!

It's a simple system. Don't change it, do it the way Scott teaches. The analytics are excellent, too, because you can look at what you're doing and see where your contacts are coming from—whether it's from specific areas of the country, specific companies, or even which particular topics are getting much activity. It's a great way to get feedback about what's working, and you'll know by the result.

Scott: Absolutely. Success leaves clues. I always tell people that you could have the recipe for chicken parmesan, but if you try to figure it out on your own and leave the cheese out, you just have a piece of chicken with some sauce. So, you need all the ingredients to get the right results.

Kelli, thank you for joining me today and sharing your takeaways. If you haven't connected with Kelli, follow her. She's amazing.

There are footprints on the beach right now waiting for all of us to walk in, so just start following them. Kelli, thank you again for being here; so grateful for you.

Summary

What I want you to take away from this is how amazing LinkedIn® can be for any business owner, entrepreneur, and especially those looking for more qualified leads, sales, and business visibility.

Here are some key things to understand:

1. LinkedIn® is 277% more effective for lead generation than Facebook®.
2. On LinkedIn®, you are allowed six times more connections than on Facebook®. You have 30,000 connections on LinkedIn®, compared to only 5000 on Facebook®.
3. The average income of someone on Facebook® and Instagram® is $30,000 per year or less, while the average income of someone on LinkedIn® is $100,000 per year or more.
4. You must look at the age demographics. The primary age demographic for someone on Facebook® and Instagram® is 18-29 years old, while LinkedIn® users tend to be 30-55 years old. This also happens to be the exact age demographic of a seasoned business owner.
5. For me, the most significant advantage of LinkedIn® is that it allows you to search, connect, message, and communicate with people globally—not just locally, which is the way most people are using Facebook.

If you are someone who wants to up-level your business this

year and forever, then you must use a platform that is built for networking with others, speaking to like-minded individuals, and to others who are interested in what you have to offer.

And as a gift from me to you, please go to www.scottaaron.net and claim your FREE infographic about the best way to set up your profile on LinkedIn® so you can hit the ground running.

If you are a business owner or professional looking to become an expert in your space, please check out https://www.thetimetogrow.com/expertauthority to learn more about joining our incredible group coaching program.

And lastly, always remember this, my friends:

Your failures will always open the doors to your successes.

Cheers, and I will see you all at the top!

About The Author

Internationally acclaimed and award-winning online marketer, 3x best-selling author, top podcaster, and speaker, Scott Aaron, is the go-to specialist in converting traffic, establishing connections, generating leads, creating sales, and building personal brands using LinkedIn®.

Fully immersing himself in learning LinkedIn® and social media strategies, Scott quickly gained traction as a leader in generating significant results for other entrepreneurs, online business owners, and business coaches.

Scott is passionate about helping fellow entrepreneurs succeed while organically building their network without complicated and costly marketing tactics.

His program has helped thousands experience explosive growth following his proven system and strategies.

People-focused and result-driven, Scott's strategic approach to teaching others how to create wealth online and organic traffic is the game changer when competing in a saturated digital world.

To learn more about how to work with Scott, visit him at www.scottaaron.net anytime.

Printed in Great Britain
by Amazon